The End of the Yellow Brick Road

The End of the Yellowbrick Road

Ways and Means to the Sustainable Society

Tim Beaumont

(Lord Beaumont of Whitley)

JON CARPENTER

First published 1997 by Jon Carpenter Publishing,
The Spendlove Centre, Charlbury OX7 3PQ
☎ 01608 811969
Please write or phone for our catalogue

ISBN 1 897766 36 X

Printed and bound in England by J. W. Arrowsmith Ltd., Bristol

Contents

ACKNOWLEDGEMENTS

My gratitude for assistance is due to a whole range of people, but in
particular to:

The staff of the Liberal Democrat Parliamentary Party in the House of Lords;

The staff of the Liberal Democrat Policy Department;

The members of the executive of The Green Liberal Democrats;

The staff of the House of Lords Library;

Malcolm Welchman who wrestled with my computer illiteracy;

Ed Mayo of the New Economics Foundation and Janet Unwin, who encouraged me;

My wife who tolerates me and without whom I would be like 'a pelican in the
wilderness';

And finally, those many writers whose instructive words I have quoted
throughout the book and whose ideas I have shamelessly kidnapped.

T.B.

Introduction

Old men and comets have been reverenced for the same reason; their long beards and pretences to foretell the future.

Jonathan Swift

What is to take the place of the soul- and life-destroying metaphysics inherited from the nineteenth century? The task of our generation, I have no doubt, is one of metaphysical reconstruction.

Fritz Schumacher

IN 1980 I WROTE a pamphlet, principally for the internal consumption of the Liberal Party, called *The Yellow Brick Road*. Reading it again recently, I was amazed at how little the main arguments seemed to have dated, the main difference today being that I have a host of authorities to consult which were then not yet on the horizon. In this book I want to explore that metaphor a little further.

When Dorothy (played in the film *The Wizard of Oz* by the incomparable Judy Garland) sets off with her companions down the yellowbrick road which, we are presumably invited to think, is at least metaphorically paved with gold, she is heading for the Emerald City to see the Wizard of Oz.[1]

But when she gets to her destination, the Emerald City proves only to seem to be Emerald because she has put on the green glasses which are obligatory for all visitors. The Wizard turns out to be an ordinary man armed with the latest technological inventions and although he does 'work the miracles' of giving the Scarecrow brains, the Tinman a heart and the Lion courage, he does it only by cosmetic operations which persuade the recipients that something has been done and which therefore give them the self-confidence to use the gifts that they have had all along. It is, I think, a very suitable parable for modern people on the road of economic growth.

This book which you are now reading is meant to be a prophetic book in both the main senses of the adjective. In the first and most common sense it deals with what is going to happen in the future or, to be more accurate, the courses which the human inhabitants of this planet are bound to take if they are not to trigger off a disaster of truly cataclysmic proportions. To try to be prophetic in this sense of the word is of course to court disaster. As G.K.

Chesterton, whom I will be quoting often, remarked, 'The human race, to which so many of my readers belong, have been playing at children's games from the beginning. And one of the games to which it is most attached is called 'Cheat the Prophet'. The players listen very respectfully and carefully to all that the clever men have to say about what is to happen in the next generation. The players then wait until all the clever men are dead and bury them nicely. They then go and do something else. That is all. For a race of simple tastes, however it is great fun.'[2]

But the other sense of the word prophecy is that it makes a moral judgement as to which course we should take. The opening gambit of the Old Testament Prophets was not the ambiguities of Delphi but the totally unambiguous 'Thus saith The Lord' and what the Lord said was almost invariably an unpalatable challenge: 'Today, I offer you the choice of life and good or death and evil...I offer you the choice of life or death, blessing or curse.'[3]

And also, because prophecy is of its nature a theological concept, it takes for granted that what should happen is more than likely to happen (one way or another, so perhaps the Delphic Oracle was in the right mould) because that is what God or the First Cause or the spirit of evolution means to happen. In which case, as Christopher Hollis once remarked, 'The job of the practical politician, as every practical politician knows, is to give names to what is happening and to persuade people to vote for the inevitable.'[4]

This double use of the concept of prophecy is the first cornerstone of this book.

Although I have done my best to keep Christian presuppositions out of the text, not least because of the ghetto into which religious publishing has largely been forced, it will probably only be read profitably by those who think that there is some purpose in life, and possibly only by those who believe that human beings have a special responsibility for the planet. (But this may be a pessimistic view; a friend of mine who tells me that he sees no purpose in life, is deeply involved as a campaigner for the objects advocated by this book.)

And what I have to say fits in with (although it does not depend on) the theory of Professor Robert W. Fogel[5] that American Society has gone through a series of moral 'awakenings' of which we are now in the fourth. It is true that he pinpoints the start of this one as the political efforts of 'the moral majority' (!) but his theory is flexible and incorporates also a Democratic revival (noting that Clinton and Gore are both Southern Baptists). Given that Gore is fundamentally green[6] in his politics I have little difficulty in seeing how my prophecies fit into his pattern.

My thesis therefore ought to be acceptable to, in the sense that its argument can be profitably followed by, all those who subscribe to the great monotheistic religions together with those who see life as having a purpose and therefore either believe in a Creator God or, while feeling unable to use that terminology, nevertheless accept the main arguments which stem from that belief.

It will also be clear that I am writing from my background on the left of politics and specifically in the tradition of the radical wing of the Liberal Party, now (in my view not very helpfully) called the Liberal Democrat Party. This background has given me a classical Liberal belief in the value of personal liberties and also in the importance of maximising what that fine Liberal thinker Ralf Dahrendorf has called 'life chances',[7] which are the sum of those choices which are, in practical terms, open to one at any given time. Until about 1920, for instance, no woman in Britain had the choice as to whether she should take a university degree or not. Afterwards, if she was rich and/or clever enough that 'life chance' became available to her. After the Second World War the necessity of being rich disappeared for a short while. The provision of such life chances for all involves in most cases the abolition of extreme economic inequality, and is important in the formation of a coherent society.

A belief in the importance of life chances for a worthwhile society is the other cornerstone of this book.

But my belief in the importance of both personal liberties and life chances leads me to reject the economic individualism, attributed by many to Adam Smith, rightly rejected by Keynes, at one time certainly part of the intellectual furniture of at least one strand of my party and later hijacked by Sir Keith Joseph, Mrs Thatcher and the economic gurus who informed them.

I also reject the authoritarianism which would say that since the ecological crisis is so acute only draconian measures will do and that, in the absence of working voluntary measures, compulsory abortions will have to be part of population control as in China. It may be so and I recognise the logic of those who are hold to the Gaian thesis that Earth is a self-supporting mechanism which will shake the human race off if it has to — and no harm done.[8] But I will not go along that path myself. The preservation of the planet without humankind does not in any way engage my sympathy or co-operation.

James Lovelock, the author of the Gaian thesis, says that we must not cling to the illusion that we could be stewards of the spaceship Earth, partly because we do not know enough and partly because we are intelligent carnivores prone to tribal genocide and, being therefore like leopards, cannot change our spots.[9] He may be right but I do not think that in practice we have any moral alternative but to attempt to act as stewards, whether we think we are employed by God, or by future generations, or by Gaia herself.

It is indeed true that we are intelligent carnivores prone to tribal genocide but one basic element in that description is that we are intelligent. (Being carnivores is certainly something about which we have a choice. Although I myself feel no ethical imperative to give up eating meat altogether (as opposed to eating less meat, for which there is a strong ecological case), many people do. And while it would be a rash person who said that we could easily give up tribal genocide, nevertheless from time to time large sections of us do so under the influence, at least partly, of some religious or other ethical imperative.

This background should make my arguments capable of being accepted, or at least admitted into rational debate, by all on a political spectrum from the far left through to that mainstream of the Conservative Party which lives up to that name and which was predominant in the generation of my father (who was Conservative MP for Aylesbury from 1929-38).

The Conservative philosopher Russell Kirk has proposed six first principles of conservatism which can be summed up as belief in:

1) a transcendent moral order;

2) social continuity (better the devil you know…);

3) the wisdom of our ancestors;

4) the importance of being guided by prudence;

5) the incurable fallibility of human nature; and

6) an affection for the proliferating intricacy of long-established social institutions.

Any Conservatives who still hold to this creed, and many do, will in most matters find themselves more at home in this book than in the creeds of the Conservative Party as it was up until 1997.

My attempts to isolate my underlying beliefs (revealed in this preface) from my detailed arguments (displayed in the rest of the book) break down, of course, when it comes to my selection of quotations. Readers will find what they may regard as an oversupply of citations from writers such as Chesterton and Schumacher who share with me a commitment to the basic message of Christianity. This is because my arrogance (though considerable) breaks down at a certain point. This book, like every other, is a patchwork of other people's ideas. The usual procedure, which for the most part I have adopted, is to disguise them as my own. But for a number of compelling reasons this proves impossible with those whom one has accepted as the great masters.

And, since a preface is the right place to define at least some of the terms the writer is going to use, let us start with Chesterton's definition of 'capitalism' as 'that economic condition in which there is a class of capitalists, roughly recognisable and relatively small, in whose possession so much of the capital is concentrated as to necessitate a very large majority of the citizens serving those capitalists for a wage'.[10] It is a slightly dated definition of course: many who have wages are capitalists according to that definition, although I think that Chesterton might have gone on (and I certainly do) to say that the capitalist class is properly seen as those who have money and who use it as capital to breed more money. Also Chesterton only just saw a day when the capitalist class could not find enough work for the citizens to perform for it. But nevertheless as a definition it will serve.

It would be idle to pretend that this book is not in a way distributist. But distributism is not entirely Chestertonian; it can be found in the teaching of the young Luther and in Cobbett.[11] Indeed there is an unlikely confluence with Thatcherism and the ideal of a 'property-owning democracy'. But the more people who claim that the road one is following is the right road, the more likely it is that the further along it you travel you will find it to be thronged with fellow pilgrims, many of them coming from unexpected directions.

It is not a thesis of this book that we should not be following a yellowbrick road to an Emerald City. It is merely that I seek to persuade you that the bricks are not made of precious metal and that the city at the end of it only appears to be made of precious, as opposed to useful, stone when you are wearing special distorting spectacles. Those who follow it out of greed are doomed to be disappointed But at least you are following a road, a road laid down for you and for others, built by Munchkins or Wizards or even witches. And to follow a road gives you more confidence than starting out in an uncharted wilderness entirely by yourself. It means that other human beings have been there before you.

On the other hand, starting work by himself is what Andy Cobham, the hero, does in Arnold Wesker's interesting political play *Their Very Own and Golden City*.[12] He has a vision of what the ideal city would be like. And it is not entirely an arrogant vision since, in spite of his faith in his own gifts as an architect, he knows that the plans must be subject to the co-operative planning of those who are going to live in it (and even of those who are putting up the capital!).

But his enterprise is doomed to failure. Six golden cities are planned, only one is finished and it is clear by the end of the play that the others will be aborted. But it is terrible work for those who have shared the vision. It was born from inside the trade union movement but the movement will not go along with it because it breaks all the rules which they have found necessary for the accomplishment of their more mundane aims (for which their members have paid their subscriptions). It catches the fancy of capital but it is spared the final degradation of being taken over by Disney Inc.[13] And I think that it becomes clear at the end of the play, though this is not explicit and may not have been intended, that the one city which finally is built is more like Welwyn Garden City or Hampstead Garden Suburb than Blake's Jerusalem (and maybe that is a more human achievement than the one which Andy had in mind. We have seen the dreadful end results of too many fine visions in our time not to settle for human-scale solutions.)

And that is a moral for those of us who toil on the ecological society of the future. We are not building something seen as 'precious' or even, like Le Corbusier's Chandigargh, as ideologically correct. Nor will it be like the hotel/casino at Las Vegas which features a Yellowbrick Road and mechanised Munchkins. It will be more like a city planned by Frank Lloyd Wright, one which fits into the landscape in which it is built. It will be practical, and it will be built and planned by human-beings 'remembering the words of Nehemiah the Prophet: "The trowel in hand, and the gun rather loose in the holster".'[14]

I choose to call that city 'civilisation' (see Chapter 1) and to write on the assumption that it is what most of us would be happy to see at the end of *our* yellowbrick road, and that many of us recognise it as being (more or less and with considerable variations) the destination at the end of the road entered through the gate called 'strait'.[15]

And, although there will be plenty of people who will oppose what I believe is going to happen, most will go along because they will recognise inevitability when they meet it and because most of us want to be seen to be on the side of the angels. John Le Carré's arms dealer who is prepared openly to avow his belief in the cause of Mammon is barely credible: 'I don't give a fart. The difference between me and the other charlies is I admit it. If a horde of niggers — yes, I said niggers, I meant niggers — if these niggers shot each other dead with my toys tomorrow and I made a bob out of it, it's great news by me. Because if I don't sell them the goods, some other charlie will. Government used to understand that. If they've gone soft, tough titty on them.'[16]

People don't think like that any longer. Or do they? They certainly don't talk like that. And how many of them act like that? Quite a number. But they act like that partly because they think that they are conforming to reality. And a couple of hundred years of the so-called Enlightenment has helped them think that way. If reality is as this book believes it is, then fewer of them will act like that in future.

1   *The Wonderful Wizard of Oz* by Frank Baum (1900). (My and Dorothy's Yellow Brick Road is not to be confused with the brothel of the same name in Manila once presided over by my one-time fellow-Liberal peer Lord Moynihan.)
2   The opening words of *The Napoleon of Notting Hill* by G.K. Chesterton (1904).
3   Deuteronomy ch 30.
4   I have used this quotation so often in political speeches (and lectures about politics) that I have mislaid the provenance and almost certainly corrupted the quotation (although not the sense). It is most likely to come from *Death of a Gentleman* (Burns and Oates 1943), that definitive, though fictional, portrait of what it was like to be a Conservative gentleman in the period up to and including the Second World War. It is interesting to compare and contrast Christopher Hollis' homespun hero Robert Fossett with fellow

Roman Catholic Evelyn Waugh's convoluted Guy Crouchback in the *Sword of Honour* trilogy.

5   'The Fourth Great Awakening' (article in *The Wall Street Journal*, 9/1/96, by Professor Robert W. Fogel of the University of Chicago School of Business.

6   *Earth in the Balance* by Al Gore (Earthscan 1992).

7   *Life Chances* by Ralf Dahrendorf (Weidenfeld/University of Chicago Press 1979).

8   James Lovelock: *Gaia: A New Look at Life on Earth* (Oxford University Press 1979).

9   Lovelock: Ch 5 of *The Precautionary Principle*, ed O'Riordan & Cameron.

10   *The Outline of Sanity* by G. K. Chesterton, Ch 1.

11   Distributism can still (just) be found in the list of political parties represented in Glasgow University Union.

12   *New British Dramatists 10* (Penguin).

13   For another of many fictional accounts of rearguard actions against Mammon read *One Man Show* (Abacus 1995), the excellent novel about modern art and the Tate Gallery by Christopher Green.

14   *Choruses from 'The Rock' V* by T. S. Eliot (1934).

15   Matthew 7.13-24.

16   *The Secret Pilgrim* by John Le Carré (Hodder and Stoughton 1991).

Chapter 1

The slide from civilisation

'Of course,' said the leader of the Gadarene swine,
Rushing furiously towards the sea,
'One knows
That the rest don't really want
To come over this steep place.
But what can one do?
I often wonder', he went on, panting,
'How we were manoeuvred
Into this position.'

Richard Mallett: *Translations from the Ish*

The forgotten American towns where no one tries to impress anybody
anymore. People do not need to pay much attention to dress or
grooming because nobody else does. The primary recreational activity
is drinking, which makes most things pretty blurry by the end of the day.
It does not really matter what things look like if one cannot see them
that well anyway.

From a commentary on the pictures of Richard Prince

HANS KÜNG, THE author of definitive accounts of the three monotheistic religions which dominate the West and are amazingly influential
throughout the rest of the world, Judaism, Christianity and Islam, sees the
German concentration camps, of which he picks Auschwitz as the archetype,
as marking the end of European modernity. Governments and peoples have
often been guilty of equally revolting savagery throughout history but the
atrocities of the Nazi regime were perpetrated in cold blood as the logical
solution to a perceived problem. They were perversions of the age of enlightenment and science and were the fruit of what was thought to be civilisation.
'European nihilism fulfilling the prophecies of Nietzsche finally made its
dramatic breakthrough and showed its empty grimace in the Nazism of
Hitler.'[1]

From Harvey Road to genocide via suicide and insanity

Undoubtedly we could choose alternative landmarks but Auschwitz is as adequate as any and better than most as a tombstone to mark the final burial (or indeed cremation) of the optimism which ruled the West up to the outbreak of the First World War. That optimism, which was common to Christians and non-Christians alike, proclaimed that humans (either powered by the grace of God or under their own steam) were mastering science, were perfecting the formulas of civilisation, and would undoubtedly continue to improve the lot of all as 'the great world rings forever down the ringing grooves of change'.

The exact formulas for how this was to be achieved varied from nation to nation and from culture to culture but the Anglo-Saxon version common to both Bloomsbury and Boston could be summed up in what Roy Harrod, the biographer of Keynes, has called 'the presuppositions of Harvey Road'.[2]

These presuppositions included the following: 'reform was achieved by the discussion of intelligent people; public opinion must be wisely guided; the government of Britain [or of the Commonwealth of Massachusetts and the United States of America] would be in the hands of an intellectual aristocracy using the method of persuasion'.[3]

Alasdair MacIntyre in his important work *After Virtue* has suggested that one of the essential tools for attaining civilisation is 'an adequate sense of tradition [which] manifests itself in a grasp of those future possibilities which the past has made available to the present. Its presence or absence manifests itself in the ability to select among the relevant stock of maxims and apply them in particular situations. Cardinal Pole possessed it, Mary Tudor did not; Montrose possessed it, Charles I did not. What Pole and Montrose possessed were those virtues which enabled them to pursue both their own good and the good of the tradition of which they were the bearers in situations of tragic dilemmatic choice'.[4]

Although this tradition of how to administer a developing civilisation still underlies the thinking and actions of the majority of those who are most admired today by the intelligentsia of the West it is clearly not grounded in any optimism. It is still thought that this is how the world *ought* to be run. But it is sadly conceded that in a world which can contain the likes of Hitler, Stalin, Pol Pot, Idi Amin and Saddam Hussein it is not likely to be how it is run as a general rule. The most that can be hoped for is that the products of Harvey Road will manage the retreat into barbarism and possible ecological disaster in a gentlemanly (and ladylike) way. And Alisdair MacIntyre goes so far as to suggest that the only way open for us is something akin to the role of the monasteries in the Dark Ages, keeping the good traditions alive in small enclaves in the midst of barbarism. That would be a possible scenario if it were not that the natural world is being destroyed about us. The damage done by the last period which we call the Dark Ages was limited; this time it may be unlimited.[5]

There are manifest signs everywhere of the crumbling of 'civilisation'. Many of the detailed figures are arguable and many which are quoted will eventually be proved to be incorrect for, in what we are increasingly and truthfully told is a global economy, global figures cannot, of their very nature, be very accurate. But the general trends are quite clear. The UN agencies tell us that the rise in world crime is at a rate of 5% per annum. The growth of the great cities continues (nine million Mexican peasant farmers have been forced off the land in the last thirty years) and as they grow they spawn unskilled, jobless underclasses of mammoth proportions which naturally drift into crime, lacking anything else to make their lives either profitable or interesting. And indeed the members of these underclasses not only drift into crime; but the most able of them are *drawn* in, since criminal gangs are the most cohesive, rewarding and appealing groups in their communities.

The best of science fiction is always worth the attention of the student of world affairs, not because its scenarios necessarily prove accurate — for, as we have seen, G.K. Chesterton has pointed out that what the human race really enjoys is not so much stoning the prophets as defeating their forecasts — but because by looking at their extrapolation of current trends we can inform the choices before us in the real world. In this context, among the best and most pertinent SF of our time is the *Neuromancer, Count Zero, Mona Lisa Overdrive* trilogy of William Gibson which describes a future world full of megacities dominated by Mafia-type organisations, trading in human body parts to correct the effects of drug dependency, where the only outlet for creative human energy is surfing the Internet. The first volume dates from 1986 and over the last ten years the human race does not appear to be defeating this particular prophet!

Another place where we should look for signs of the decline of civilisation is in the figures relating to suicide and mental illness, the former of which so often has its roots in the anomie attributed by Emile Durkheim to the 'disintegration of a commonly accepted normative code'. It is particularly worrying for example that in the UK student suicides have risen by 400% over ten years.[6]

Or, if we turn from suicide to terrorism, which is merely to change the target of human violence, Khaled Kelkal, the Paris Metro bomber who was shot dead by the police at the age of 24, had found no one in authority during his life (which was indeed 'solitary, poor, nasty, brutish and short') who would listen or speak to him. His school was big and impersonal, the clerks at the labour exchanges treated him as a cypher whose ambitions were of no conceivable interest, he visited his town hall several times but the mayor would never see him. So he determined to be heard and eventually he was!

And the number of the mentally ill is escalating. When I first took over the magazine *Time and Tide* in the early sixties we relaunched it with rather a good advertising campaign. At least we thought it was good until the first ad landed us up before the Press Council who rightly protested that when we announced as a banner headline that 'The Chances are 10 to 1 that You Will Go Mad', meaning as we carefully explained in the small type that one in ten of the population suffered from mental illness at some stage of their life, we had got our betting terminology wrong and the odds were the other way round. I have quoted those (corrected) figures ever since until someone gently brought me up to date the other day and pointed out that now, thirty years later, the figures have doubled and that one in every five people in Britain are now treated for mental illness at some time in their lives.

Another sign of the growing size of the problem is the increasingly obvious inability of even large non-governmental organisations (NGOs) to tackle the short-term problems brought to their attention. Governmental organisations (national, regional and world) are not able to do much except on a major scale (the possibilities and dangers of which I will examine later) and Oxfam, Christian Aid, Cafod and the like are increasingly driven to tackling problems on a very small scale and locally which, as I also argue, is demonstrably right, but its very rightness tends to stand as a witness to the growing magnitude of the problems such a strategy is hardly able to scratch.

Another measure of the failure if not the actual decline of civilisation might be found in the breaches of the Universal Declaration of Human Rights passed unanimously by the UN in 1948. Article 25 says: 'Everyone has the right to a standard of living adequate for the health and well-being of himself and his family, including food, clothing, housing and medical care and necessary social services, and the right to security in the event of unemployment, sickness, disability, widowhood, old age or other lack of livelihood'. There is probably nowhere in the world, with the possible exception of Scandinavia and some small islands, where this article is not seriously breached every day, not excluding the UK and the US (where the Declaration is held up constantly as a goal for other countries to achieve before they are worthy of American help and friendship).

Symptoms: art, sport and complexity

Nor is it only in the field of the purely material that we find this slide from 'civilisation'. The fragmentation of modern art has something to say to us in this context. I am married to someone who writes and lectures on the subject of modern art and our house is full of examples of the genre, a few of which I chose or bought myself and most of which I understand and appreciate, so that I am fully aware of the dangers of pontificating and making too-facile judgements in the manner of the late Sir Alfred Munnings.

But I remember going with a group to Barcelona several years ago. The first objective of our visit was to see the architecture of Gaudi, especially the unfinished cathedral dedicated to 'La Sagrada Familia'. That is one of those buildings which give me 'the authentic frisson' of sheer aesthetic pleasure combined with a primeval fear of the 'holy'. But in the same trip, under the auspices of The British Council, on whose Executive I then sat as one of the three party political representatives, a lecturer from the Tate, who is both an agreeable friend and a highly competent art historian, gave a slide lecture on the contemporary show at the Tate. The evening started off on an unfortunate note when, as the young anglophile art aficionados of Barcelona were filing in in considerable numbers, the British Council representative was heard to say in a loud voice that all art ended as far as he was concerned with Gainsborough. And it continued on a worse one when the slide projector proved to date from roughly the same period and, consequently, it was very difficult to fit the slides into their proper slots. As a result the assistant handling the projector panicked and made a large number of errors.

Now if the lecture had been about Gainsborough the resulting problems would have been relatively easy to shrug off. But it so happened that the main Tate exhibit which was being shown was an installation of photographs of a clock depicting the passing of time at five minute intervals. The lecturer coped very well but an exhibition which, when displayed in the Tate in a large silent gallery, enabled one to muse on the nature of art, time and other imponderables, had totally other effects when the photographs appeared in the wrong order (thus destroying the time sequence) and sometimes upside down or reversed (making an entirely different although possibly valid point about the nature of time).

As a result the audience were divided between hilarity and bewilderment. Not entirely sure that they knew modern art when they saw it, but willing to learn, they had all possible reference points removed from them. That was an illustration of the fragility of modern art when it comes into collision with Murphy's Law but even when not accident prone it can leave one floundering. In a recent article in *Art Review*,[7] that sympathetic and prolific critic Edward Lucie-Smith pointed out that a 15th or 16th century artist who showed the audience a Pietà, with the dead Christ lying in his mother's lap, could count on an immediate recognition of his subject which then gave him the freedom to use the nuances of his painting to deliver an immediate and unique message. But visitors to a recent Whitney Biennial in New York, for example, were greeted immediately they emerged from the fourth floor elevator by a work which consisted of 'a mass of dilapidated mattresses, rolled up, roped together and hung from the ceiling'. On closer inspection they found that the interstices of these mattresses were 'filled with squashed cakes' from a commercial bakery and that the accepted explanation of this sculpture is that it is about the homeless who live on mattresses and were, according to legend, instructed by Marie Antoinette, when she was told that they had no bread, to eat cake.

Now the moral of these stories is not that what is being shown is not 'art', since presumably 'art' is what the 'artist' decides is art, nor that the artist would be better employed in a factory or on the farm because today neither factories nor farms would have jobs for him. But it is surely a commentary on the nature of modern 'civilisation' that its art is so chaotic and (for many artists, though not the best) out of touch with its own traditions.

The fine art publisher in Michael Ayrton's fascinating novel about Picasso[8] says: 'Those who wish to be up to date in the visual arts still find the past embarrassing... They are like prospectors participating in a gold rush who know no more about mining than to seek for nuggets, broken away from the lode, which they hope to beat into simple shapes which will prove to be new inventions'.

Sport

Sport is sport. It is not a business or entertainment.
Peter Thomson, five times winner of the Open Golf Championship

And if art is an area where present 'civilisation' seems to have become divorced from its roots and power to communicate, sport is another. Sport has historically been played because men and women appreciate bodily excellence and skill in themselves and in others. It flourishes because it proves that such excellence is attainable. Without being diverted into a discussion as to whether the making of golf courses is a proper use of land today, almost every golfer, however bad, has at one time or another played a perfect shot. And every one of them knows that that was, in miniature, a fulfilment of their humanity worthy of celebration at the nineteenth hole.

But how far is that removed from 'a world game that lasts for eleven months as players circle the globe in search of tournaments, prize money and lucrative sponsorship deals,' while breaking up their marriages along the way?[9]

And even horse racing, which did start as a competition to see not 'whether one horse could go faster than another', because you do not have to be a sophisticate to know that, but 'whether one particular horse belonging to a particular person could go faster than another particular horse belonging to another particular person', has now become a sport in which 'an owner is invited to bring his wife and his trainer and his wife, and his jockey and his wife, all of whom are sent club-class tickets, given free accommodation and food in a leading hotel with presents and parties and outings'[10] in a distant part of the world, all of which uses up the world's resources, in order to discover the same thing.

The effects of capitalism on civilisation

Money is only a medium of exchange.   John Stuart Mill

As we look at such symptoms of the decline of civilisation we come, I believe, to see that part of both the cause and the effect is the overwhelming power of unbridled capitalism with its emphasis on quantitative growth and its debasing effect on quality and diversity.

And our 'civilisation' begins to find itself adrift when it discovers that quantitative growth cannot go on for ever. Just as a moment comes when we spend more real resources getting rid of the wrapping paper than we gain from the present, so another sign of insanity is when there are so many gadgets that they interfere with each other. As I write, there is a report that some mobile telephones used in cars (essential to ensure that the drivers have no time to look at any scenery that may be left) activate the car's complex brake system bringing the car to a shuddering halt in the middle of the motorway (and the conversation). By the time you read this that particular glitch will almost certainly have been ironed out. But the ironing out itself will cost resources and, in any case, I mention it to record a symptom, not the disease itself.

So if the 'civilisation' which gave us the Bloomsbury Group also gave us Belsen[11] and is showing all these minor symptoms of illness, what has gone wrong with it? In order to answer that question we should examine more closely what it is that should make up civilisation.

As a starting point we need go no further than a definition provided by W.H. Auden. Civilisation, he once remarked, is a combination of the aesthetic, the religious and the practical so that each has its place and all three influence each other. If we accept that definition — and I do — our only reaction to twentieth-century Anglo-Saxon 'civilisation' must be the same as that of Gandhi who, when arriving in London in the thirties, was asked by a reporter what he thought of civilisation and replied: 'That would be a good idea.'

Where then does our civilisation fail? The strongest point of its triangle, if we apply Auden's definition, is clearly the 'practical' one. That, at least, is what those who are its most sturdy defenders would claim. Looking round the world, we may beg leave to doubt it, but we can see that they have a point. At least the Germany of Hitler, which we have pinpointed as the turning point of 'modern civilisation', was until 1939 a model of practicality. Its renaissance really did deserve that much abused label 'an economic miracle' and, by at the same time solving unemployment and building the Autobahns, the predecessors of those monuments to 'practicality', the motorway systems of the world, it showed that it was 'civilised'.

The creation of an underclass

But even on the practical front our present civilisation seems now to be failing. The exclusion of large numbers of our citizens from most of what makes up society, those who are now commonly referred to as 'the underclass', is wrong ethically, aesthetically and practically. To put the argument at its most practical, capitalism demands markets and the underclass has not enough money to be a good market, while the rich, once they have satisfied their real needs, spend their money on goods and services which give ever more marginal satisfaction and which, as R.H. Tawney pointed out, entail a perpetual misdirection of resources to the production of costly futilities, thus not realising the potential wealth of the world. And to those who argue, as classical economists tend to, that there is no better way to find out what people believe that they need than the market, the answer is that that might well be true if all people had roughly equivalent purchasing power, but is certainly not true with the present distribution of wealth.

(It is of course ironic that the world's final verdict on socialism as a way of establishing the needs of people and then satisfying them, which is that 'the collapse of the Soviet Empire proves that socialism does not work', comes at a time when the revolution in information technology would make it possible for a central planning authority to respond sensitively to peoples needs and indeed would help them to make decisions which had larger horizons than those the market system can provide).

The result of all this is that even in the rich world a city like 'New York, a major centre of economic power, manifest[s] all the qualities of a contemporary Third World city — including wandering armies of the homeless juxtaposed with the extravagant lifestyles of the rich and famous, incapacitated government and indiscriminate violence'.[12]

The need for ethics and aesthetics

But, working backwards through Auden's trinity, we move from practicality to religion. I think there is little doubt that religion in the widest sense is essential to a civilisation; indeed T.S. Eliot, in *Notes Towards the Definition of Culture*, in which he maintains that the definitions of culture and civilisation overlap to a large degree, argues that cultures and civilisations only come into being (and stay in being) when associated with a religion. And when we examine the decay of modern civilisation it is clear that the religious element is one which is certainly lacking. This is no place to look at the religious scene of the developed world today, except just to note that no one, from whatever standpoint, would call it healthy. And if we look once again at Hitler's Germany we find that even he realised the need for this element but that it failed to perform its proper function, since instead of choosing one of the ethically advanced religions (which would of course not have served his purposes) he cobbled up a Nietzschean Wagnerian substitute which led to Belsen and the Götterdämmerung of the Berlin bunker.

And it may well be in this need for a religion that we can include the need for the new public philosophy of 'responsibility' for citizens called for by Ralf Dahrendorf (and many, many others).[13]

For the religion of the capitalist way of life is the worship of Mammon (Marx quite rightly pointed out that capitalism tears apart social ties and substitutes 'universal exchange relations'). And Mammon is not a very satisfactory God. There are parts of us he cannot in fact reach; 'Thou hast created us for thyself, and our heart cannot be quieted till it may find repose in thee'[14] wrote St Augustine, and Harry Williams comments that 'our wanting more in fact goes deeper than anything that our earthly environment can supply'.[15]

It is worth noting here that when we come to consider whether the new ecological paradigm (which, I will argue, is already upon us) fulfils Auden's definition we may decide that it does in itself contain a major element which we cannot help seeing as religious. To say that is not to say that it will replace other religions. Indeed the work already done in this field by the Alliance of Religions and Conservation (ARC) the World Wildlife Fund (with its Assisi Declaration) and ICOREC (the International Consultancy on Religion, Education and Culture) is enough to show that all the major religions — Buddhism, Christianity, Hinduism, Islam, Judaism, Sikhism and Baha'i — will move easily into a new paradigm based on the needs of the universe and that this paradigm will become a lynchpin of inter-faith dialogue. This is not to say that there will be no awkward moments; the present official attitude of the Roman Catholic Church to artificial contraception is enough to demonstrate that. But they ought to be surmountable; the present attitude and behaviour of ordinary members of the Roman Catholic Church in developed countries to the same topic is enough to demonstrate that too.

And if this is so then MacIntyre's forecast of a new dark age may prove to be over-pessimistic. MacIntyre, we may recall, told us that 'what matters at this stage is the construction of local forms of community within which civility and the intellectual and moral life can be sustained through the new dark ages which are already upon us. This time however the barbarians are not waiting beyond the frontiers; they have already been governing us for some time. And it is our lack of consciousness of this that constitutes part of our predicament. We are not waiting for Godot, but for another — doubtless very different — St Benedict.'[16] The ecological imperative may perform exactly that role.

And thirdly in our analysis of civilisation we come to the aesthetic element. Here there is more question for argument since *de gustibus non disputandum*, which, being roughly translated, means 'you can go on disputing for ever about what is disgusting'. But there would be wide agreement, first with Edward Lucie-Smith (see above) on the void caused by the fragmentation of modern art, and second with the overwhelming consensus that attempts like those of fascism in its various forms to resist modern art show little except sterility of taste. Or, if we look at architecture, we find the path through the Bauhaus leading to what we might call a brick wall (if there were any likelihood at all of it being made with bricks instead of reinforced concrete) in the form of dehumanising slabs of modernism, succeeded in their turn if not by the nihilistic aesthetic of the pictorial arts, since the redeeming feature of architecture is that it has, in almost all cases a purpose beyond itself, then by a post-modernism which may in its eclecticism provide a counterpart to the philosophical move away from Cartesianism which is at the heart of ecological economics.

A civilisation which takes religion and aesthetics seriously as Auden and Eliot would have us do will certainly be one which does not value trade for trade's sake. The more worldwide trade there is, the more we will get what has been termed 'homogenisation by instant mass-communication', not to mention the destructive effect it will have on species diversity which thrives on diversity of habitats which, in their turn, are caused not just by geography and climate but also by the patterns of human activity.

The fact is that we have achieved a state of affairs, in the words of Yosef Gotlieb 'where increasing environmental instability, social unrest and maladaptive economies are forging a set of unbearable stresses that will affect the industrialised North no less than the less developed South'. He goes on to detail a number of the symptoms of global economic instability, listing as his first seven:

(1) growing income disparities within and among societies;

(2) the foreign debt crisis;

(3) the inability of the 'absolute poor' to meet daily subsistence needs

(4) concentration of capital and control over capital and production factors by elites and TNCs;

(5) distortions in labor utilization (scarcity, unemployment, underemployment);

(6) the failure to cost the value of environmental resources (particularly of stock resources) in production; and

(7) heightened speculation in capital as a commodity.[17]

Is there then any way in which we can create a true (balanced) civilisation starting from where we are now, one which does not end in the fate of Midas

— for what does it benefit you if everything you touch turns to gold, and therefore so do your sons and daughters?

One of the steps necessary if we are to live in a truly civilised world is to achieve a balance which can produce practical ends, while not abandoning the other two elements. This will involve the end not of classical economics but of their domination of our behaviour, the realisation that economics is but a subset of ecology.

1   Hans Küng: *Judaism* (SCM Press, 1991), p 589.
2   Harvey Road, Cambridge was where Keynes lived in his youth (and where, incidentally and totally irrelevantly, my wife and I first set up house after our marriage).
3   D. E. Moggridge: *Keynes* (Fontana Modern Masters 1976), p38.
4   Alisdair MacIntyre: *After Virtue* (Duckworth 1981).
5   In that brilliant book *A Canticle for Liebowitz* by Walter M. Miller Jr (Weidenfeld and Nicholson 1960), the final survivors take off by spaceship but it is doubtful whether in any imaginable scenario a spaceship would be available to those who could be entrusted with a new planet.
6   Research done by Don Foster MP (*Liberal Democrat News* 3/11/95)
7   *Art Review* June 1995, p12.
8   *The Midas Consequence* by Michael Ayrton (Secker & Warburg 1974).
9   *Times* report by John Hopkins, Oct 1995.
10 Clement Freud in *The Times,* 11/12/95.
11 If my life passed through Harvey Road (see Note 2 above) it also skirted Belsen since, when doing my National Service, I was stationed at Bergen-Belsen in the luxurious barracks built for Hitler's Panzer Regiments (so luxurious that the Wehrmacht earned a personal rebuke from the Führer for building them). The Regiment I was attached to was one of the Royal Tank Regiments, another of which first liberated the concentration camp and yet another of which finally went through it with flame throwers.
12 David Korten: *When Corporations Rule The World* (Earthscan 1995).
13 Dahrendorf: *Report on Wealth Creation.*
14 St Augustine: *Confessions,* Ch 1.
15 H. A. Williams C.R.: *The Joy of God* (Mitchell Beazley 1979), p16.
16 Alisdair MacIntyre: *After Virtue*, p261.
17 Yosef Gotlieb: *Development, Environment and Global Dysfunction*, p17.

Chapter 2

The cancer of capitalism

Those who seek the direct road to truth should not bother with any object of which they cannot have a certainty equal to the demonstrations of arithmetic and geometry.

René Descartes: *Rules for the Direction of the Mind*

The social affections' says the political economist 'are accidental and disturbing elements in human nature; but avarice and the desire for 'progress' are constant elements. Let us eliminate the inconstants, and, considering the human being merely as a covetous machine, examine by what laws of labour, purchase, and sale, the greatest accumulative result in wealth is attainable. Those laws once determined, it will be for each individual afterwards to introduce as much of the disturbing affectionate element as he chooses, and to determine for himself the result on the new conditions supposed.

John Ruskin: *Unto This Last*

Economists have run off to hide in the thickets of algebra and left the really serious problems of economic policy to be handled by journalists.

Joan Robinson, quoted by Herman Daly in *Resurgence* 175

Excessive environmentalism pollutes the economy.

American economist Sidney Rolfe

THE TRUE NATURE of capitalism as we experience it today can be best examined in the workings of classical economics. The roots of classical economics lie in Cartesian philosophy which rejects any 'good' that you cannot measure and therefore the whole concept of 'higher' and 'lower' values. As a result, those who base their work in this field tend, in the words of F.E. Smith, to be 'not wiser, my Lord, but better informed'.

The virtues of classical economics

It would be untrue to say that we do not owe a great deal to the discipline of classical economics with its variation neoclassical economics (see Chapter 4), and to the Cartesian philosophy which lies beneath it. It provided a framework which possibly stimulated the scientific discoveries of the enlightenment and certainly enabled the discoverers and their associates to turn them into easily negotiable wealth.

In dual harness with the professions (which it was later to destroy), it was able to bring us a world in which, as its defenders never cease to remind us, we could undergo painless surgical operations and make 'two ears of corn or two blades of grass to grow upon a spot of ground where only one grew before'.

And it provided the necessary conceptual framework to enable us to operate markets. Mind, I do not say 'Market', for the use of the singular and of the capital letter is a device to make us succumb to the idea that markets somehow are part of a universal law instead of being a term for a handy tool to be used for our diverse benefits. And 'The Free Market', which is the apotheosis of 'The Market', as Wendell Berry has reminded us, 'sees to it that everything ends up in the right place — that is, it makes sure that only the worthy get rich. All millionaires and billionaires, it is well known, have worked hard at increasing *our* wealth and they deserve to be rewarded for that work, for which they also need all the help that they can get from government and from the universities. It is also well known that having money stimulates the rich to further economic activity that ultimately benefits the rest of us while needing money stimulates the rest of us to further economic activity that ultimately benefits everybody'[1] (but which mysteriously seems to appear in the pockets of the rich).

We must not forget that classical economics is merely a disciplinary subset of ecology, like agriculture or science: ecology is the science (logos) of how we all live in our world and economy describes the set of instructions which will enable us to pursue certain ends (the conservation of assets) most efficiently. If we let classical economics or its creature capitalism force us to pursue those ends (as opposed to other ones such as, say, the maximisation of love) they become uncontrollable monsters, rather like the compulsive housewife who tries to keep her house so clean that living in it becomes a penance rather than a delight.

But as long as we remember that in using economics we are merely dealing with a robot servant, then the most important thing for all of us will be to discover (or remember) the nature of the household which we inhabit before we can wisely devise the rules for achieving its housekeeping.

The dangers of uncontrolled classical economics

If we do not channel or control our robot servant he can land us in a nightmare world, one example of which is beautifully illustrated in a long account in the *New Yorker* of the vodka wars.[2] Until fairly recently the vodka market in the West was dominated by the House of Smirnoff. Then the Swedish makers of Absolut vodka hired an advertising agency to mount a campaign to push their brand with the result that the shares of the market were reversed. As a result of some changes in the industry Absolut's advertising agency was later unwisely released from its contract whereupon it was promptly hired by Smirnoff and settled down to reversing its work. Not only have vast sums been wasted (and are still being wasted) in persuading people to drink one particular form of colourless, odourless form of alcohol (itself surely a dubious boon) rather than another but some of the most creative brains in the West have been employed in achieving this end.

That such a position can arise in a 'civilisation' which regards itself as reasonable is the result of the takeover of humankind by the Market and it comes of not asking the right questions.[3] There is a small but largely admirable institution in Britain called the Liberal Summer School. It was was founded by Maynard Keynes among others and, like other summer schools of its vintage, it meets every year to examine some question of note with the aid of distinguished speakers in an atmosphere where the conversation at meal times and in the bar is at least as important as the set agenda. In 1995 the Liberal Summer School met in Hull to discuss 'The Global Economy'. It proved to be on balance a good school but it started by asking the wrong question. The speakers took as their starting point the fact that we now had a global economy and asked themselves and us how we were to adapt ourselves to it, whereas the question that many of us wanted to ask (and suggested that Keynes himself would have been asking) was: given that certain developments have occurred in the housekeeping (economics) of the world, how do we harness them in order to achieve a civilised society (or more pertinently a large number of civilised societies)?

In other words we must be clear as to the ends before we can intelligently examine the means. Once we are moderately clear on the ends, we can start asking the most important questions about the means, questions which are seldom asked because it is assumed that the answers are self-evident. Answers about means which are self-evident to those who want one set of ends (or, more likely, do not even think about ends at all, regarding them as a given) are not so self-evident to those who are striving for a different and a better world.

One of the main questions which capitalism fails to ask is, 'For what purpose is money to be accumulated?' It assumes that we accumulate wealth from production in order to invest it to get more capital. In other words we want money in order to enable us to get even more money. And the more capital we can invest the more, in present conditions, we can reduce 'labour', or at least spend as little money as possible providing good conditions for those working for us.

The result can be a society in which great opulence disguises backscene barbarism, as in Peter Greenaway's film *The Cook, the Thief, the Wife and her Lover* or George Orwell's *Down and Out in Paris and London* or the refined taste of paté de foie gras produced by monstrous cruelty to geese.

God and Mammon

This co-existence of misery and luxury, which is a major feature of life in the West, is a result of our neglect of one of the few great laws of nature, compared with which all the 'laws' of economics pale into insignificance: 'You cannot serve God and Mammon'. It is not a piety; it is not a commandment, God-given or otherwise; it is a whacking great plonking statement of fact. A statement of which the principle, not the terminology, is sancrosanct; you can say 'You cannot serve Gaia and GDP' if that is your bent, or even 'You cannot serve humanity and classical economics', and it still remains true. None of the great religions of the world places the pursuit of material wealth high up its list of priorities, although all of them are quite clear that the relief of poverty and misery is important. The rock-solid truthfulness of the axiom means that the followers of Mammon or GDP or classical economics are always trying to pretend that it is not true. 'Of course you can have the best of both worlds,' they trumpet: 'It is not a question of either/or but of both/and. Mammon is a kind master and will give you time off on Sundays to go to church as long as it does not interfere with seven day a week shopping.'

But it is important to note that the quest for money tends to widen the gap between ourselves and other humans. This gap creates a feeling of alienation which advertisers then tell us that their products can assuage. And this in turn leads to the quest for more money. A really vicious circle.

That it is not a question of either/or but of both/and is a particularly engaging argument because in most not entirely fundamental questions both/and is usually a better answer than either/or. But not in this one. This is an entirely fundamental question, the $64,000 question as the followers of Mammon would say; although their opponents might phrase it differently. 'Today, I offer you the choice of life and good or death and evil... I offer you the choice of life or death, blessing or curse'.[4]

Once we have decided on which side of that argument we stand, we can start not denying or contradicting the economists but asking them the important questions which they do not seem to ask themselves. As Chesterton said, 'The modern world is filled with men who hold dogmas so strongly that they do not even know that they are dogmas'. This comes to much the same as Keynes' comment that 'Practical men who believe themselves to be quite exempt from any intellectual influences are usually the slaves of some defunct economist'. And Keynes himself took precautions against enslaving his successors. It is true that people apply some of his theories in areas where they are not applicable (and where he would not have applied them). But if we follow Keynes' methods (as opposed to his conclusions) we will not be in thrall to him, because his work was the model of what an economist who regards himself as a craftsman and not as a pedlar of divine truths ought to produce: he always asked first (a) 'What do we want to achieve?', second (b) 'What are the prevailing facts?' and only then did he (c) work out the form of housekeeping (economics) to enable him to get us from (b) to (a).

Capitalism and the use of time

It is one of the paradoxes of capitalism (and the result of another unasked question) that an ideology which sets out to 'save time' in the sense that it always wishes to reduce labour ends up by making sure that we attribute no value to time at all.

What, for instance, are we to do with the time that we have saved? We know what the employers are going to do with it; they are going to turn it into lower costs, higher profits and, just conceivably, lower prices. But what are we workers/consumers going to do with it? The latest technical gadgets are, according to the advertisers, going to buy us 'quality time' with our family. But do they? Not a bit of it: either they work us so hard that when we see our family we are unable to share their 'real' lives or they get us so used to gadgets that when we have leisure we want to employ it on other gadgets.

The movement of capital, homogeneity of civilisation, and putting the clock back

Let us look at another instance of the evils of uncontrolled capitalism in the global movement of money which, because it is virtually instantaneous, is involved in 'the abolition of time'. This global movement is now taken for granted as the norm. It has been estimated that for every \$1 circulating in the productive world economy there are \$20-50 circulating in the world of (?) pure finance.[5] And a lot of that money is circulating 'untouched by human hand' in that it is being traded by computers which obey the software they are fed! We must apparently accept this vicious nonsense. 'You can't turn the clock back,' we were repeatedly being told at the Summer School I have described. But, leaving aside Chesterton's riposte that 'of course you can, all you have to do is to stand on a chair and move the hands', it is not a self-evident proposition that we cannot undo what has been done. The idea that history is linear is recognised as just as dubious as the idea that it is circular, but there is a very strong case indeed for saying that it is spiral or cyclical and you can insert corrections in processes as they pass you by during this particular curl.

And in any case we must distinguish between 'a regression in time', which probably is impossible, and 'revising an error', which wise men do every day. After all, we now try to stage Shakespeare's plays as he wrote them rather than in the modernised versions of Cibber and Garrick. We have quite rightly and efficaciously turned the clock back in that field.

Nor is it self-evident that to correct a recent fault is to 'turn the clock back'. Books like this one are often accused of wanting to return to feudal times, when we are merely suggesting that the next step forward in social organisation will include the best of past feudalism and the best of present capitalism as well as many things which are new and some which may be at the moment unimaginable.

Indeed any change of paradigm involves moving into a different pattern of history and already perspicacious observers are noticing what look like major reversals of trends hitherto thought immutable. Niall Ferguson[6] has pointed out that the nation states are unravelling in both Eastern and Western Europe while China may well be next on the list. The social and economic reforms of Roosevelt and Attlee are also unwinding. He deduces that we are regressing to the eighteenth century with, in the UK (rapidly becoming an un-united kingdom) alternations of Whig (Blairite) and Tory placemen (quangos) complete with a Royal Family awash with scandal.

If these kinds of changes are happening, what is the authority for saying that you cannot restrain the international movement of capital? This complete freedom of capital is of recent origin. As far as Britain is concerned I have seen it referred to as one of Geoffrey Howe's achievements — and incidentally it destroys almost everything which was understood by Adam Smith and his followers to form the basis of the doctrine of comparative advantage.

That doctrine says that I trade with you because you can produce some things I want more cheaply than I can produce them, and I can produce some things you want more cheaply than you can. These comparative advantages are caused partly by the differences in the soil we live on (land) and our climate; partly because of differences in the cost of skilled labour which is still moderately immobile (although we must emphasise the qualification 'moderately' since the growth merchants are working on the extension of rootlessness); and partly because capital was deemed to be geographically static. Well, it no longer is.

One of the results of the free untrammelled movement of capital has passed beyond internationalism. William Rees-Mogg has pointed out[7] that modern technology means that money is now shifted in cyberspace and he forecasts a time within the next thirty years when no authority, national or international, will be able to get at money in order to tax it. I think that his forecasts are a little extreme since money has no value in itself; it is only a medium of exchange and has no value if it cannot be exchanged for real wealth existing in the world of tangibles, or at least in the world of know how. It is of no use if you cannot spend it. And nation states or even bloc or world governments can catch the money both where it is produced and where it is spent. It is true that the spirit of the age is such that it is not regarded as sporting to do so and California — which is having a good shot at taxing imputed income — is thought to be a spoilsport and is therefore being challenged in the courts.

But California is right. The trend which William Rees-Mogg describes undoubtedly exists and for the good of any kind of a civilised society it must be controlled. The alternative is the nightmare world of William Gibson which I have described above.

But the free untrammelled movement of capital through conventional channels has many deleterious results and even Ricardo said that he would be sorry to see the emigration of capital.[8] Nor should we ignore the fact that perhaps as much as 90% of the flow of cash is moving not for any real benefit to the community but merely in the course of speculation. 'The new global financial system works systematically in the interests of financial operators, as opposed to those of productive manufacturers or government planners', says the United Nations Research Institute for Social Development.[9] It is not just Britain which thinks it can solve problems through a National Lottery; the whole globe has become a casino with little rake-off for the common Bank. And the measure of how much we take this for granted is the ease with which the G7 group of powers shrugged off Chancellor Kohl's eminently sensible suggestion of a tax on currency trades.

But even if the free and instantaneous shifting of money about the globe was not largely performed in the interests of gambling, it would still not necessarily be a good thing. For widespread trade results in a growing reduction of life on this planet to a bland norm, an ironing out of everything distinctive and enriching or, as Chesterton put it: 'The modern world seems to have no notion of preserving different things side by side, of allowing its proper and proportionate place to each, of saving the whole varied heritage of culture. It has no notion except that of simplifying something by destroying nearly everything'.[10] It is no accident that the Viet Nam War, so far the ultimate capitalist war (as opposed to the Gulf Walkover), featured the 'liberation' of ancient cities by levelling them to the ground.

And most of us do not want an amorphous world. We are addicted to particularity. If we love England (or any other country) it is not a Platonic England which is the object of our affections, it is (in my case) the England of the ford in County Durham where the geese threatened to attack me when I was eight or the England of the total absurdity of the Palace of Westminster. And if fords (which are untidy and cause car engines to stall) and Gothic architecture (which is appallingly difficult to heat and not very easy to maintain) are going to be phased out, to suit international tastes or economic dicta, then Chesterton's remark will be proved true. And if you think that I have chosen idiotic examples which can never be attacked, a short perusal of Christopher Driver's columns in the *Sunday Telegraph* will reveal many actual examples I could have chosen. There is no point in spending much time on housekeeping if you don't want to live in that particular house. It has long been remarked that it would have been a waste of time to rearrange the deckchairs on the deck of the *Titanic* and it is equally a waste of time to do minor repairs to a house which is almost certain to be swept over the edge of the cliff in the near future, or which is being so altered under you that you no longer want to live in it.

In any case the flow of money does not do what Adam Smith described and benefit the concentration of investment in those goods in which a country can most profitably specialise. For, as Sir James Goldsmith has pointed out, it is *limitation* of capital which makes a nation concentrate on those goods where it has comparative advantage, whereas a completely free migration of money around the world tends to end up investing indiscriminately in those countries which do not have a comparative advantage in any particular product but merely a general advantage in cheap labour.[11]

If enough people want to preserve an existing form of housekeeping which suits them and which they believe will suit their successors, they can do so as long as they can persuade enough of their peers within a nation state (or any other more-or-less sovereign community). And if we want to control the free flow of capital around the world, we can. And to get it to control itself is probably even more effective, provided that we ensure that the people retain ultimate control and that self-regulation does not include the power to abandon all regulation as soon as greed takes control of the regulators.

The insurance industry already exercises considerable control over the investment objectives of transnational corporations (TNCs) because it is quite clear now that there are ventures which no one in their right mind would insure (the members of Lloyds of London having been demonstrably shown not to be in their right minds and thus serving as a useful object lesson). Such ventures are those which do such damage to the environment that, in a world where people and corporations are being held increasingly liable to pay for all the damage that they inflict, insurance premiums would be impossibly high.

And if the insurance companies have enough clout to defend the environment in their own interests, then nation states (if enough of them agree) have still enough power, both legislative and persuasive, to control what is going on. It is not in the interests of TNCs to battle against any opponents who are not considerably weaker than themselves.

Riches the enemy of wealth

> Let none admire [wonder]
> That riches grow in Hell; that soil may best
> Deserve the precious bane.
>
> John Milton

It is exactly right that it is in *Paradise Lost* that Milton points out the surprisingly poisonous nature of riches, because it is precisely in destroying *wealth* that riches cause Paradise to be Lost.

Perhaps here it is worth reminding ourselves of Ruskin's definitions of wealth, money and riches: '"Wealth" consists of things in themselves valuable [and Garrett Hardin[12] tells us that those things come in only three forms: matter, energy and information], "Money" consists of documentary claims to the possession of such things; and "Riches" is a relative term expressing the magnitude of the possessions of one person or society as compared with those of other persons or societies'.[13]

Money can never be an end in itself, except for misers; it is only a means and all who pursue it for its own sake will find it unrewarding. Most people want to live in a healthy and prosperous society and no society with great extremes of rich and poor is healthy; it is always under threat of disruption, nor has it its full capability of investment, even if we judge it on capitalism's own terms. It is one of the platitudes of modern economies — and unlike most of the platitudes of modern economies, this one is actually true — that economic progress depends on savings and investment.

All the high-performing Asian economies have had exceptionally high rates of saving and investment. The reasons for these high rates have largely been (a) political stability and (b) a reasonably equal distribution of income (which you may think are interconnected) resulting to some extent from the radical land reforms of the late 1940s.[14] A reasonably equitable distribution of income within a society leads to political stability because it avoids the battle between the haves and the have nots which is exacerbated by extremes.

The Rawlsian definition of a fair society as one into which we would choose to be born if we did not know into what stratum of it we might be pitchforked is also a good definition of a society which will be at ease with itself. And a society which is also intragenerationally fair is one which satisfies both society's conscience and its emotional investment in its children.

You may think that in urging actions, such as saving, which enable growth of GNP I am forgetting that I have rejected that kind of growth as a worthwhile objective. But in fact much the same factors as aid the growth of GNP will aid the growth of true wealth. For it is investment in the devices which will enable us to use our resources frugally and dispose of our excreta safely and economically that will enable us to maximise those things which we decide will provide us with the good life.

So, if we want a truly wealthy society we will create one which invests and one which is at ease with itself because it has abolished extremes of poverty and wealth. It will also be a society which is good at accounting and makes sure that it pays its way. One of the reasons why our economics are so askew is our failure to understand all the costs we are imposing on the planet and on society. If we took into account the true costs of transport, including the pollution of the air and the diminution of the ozone layer, we would not so easily leap to the conclusion that trade was necessarily a good thing.

The dangers of trade and travel

In the days when parts of the world were in infrequent touch with one another there was a stronger case than there is at the moment for the growth in international trade. The international contacts which came from quinquiremes of Nineveh from distant Ophir, rowing home to haven in sunny Palestine, caused little environmental damage although we may query whether cargoes of apes and peacocks would be seen as a good thing today or whether they seriously benefited anyone very much then.

But it is clear that a dirty British coaster with a salt-caked smokestack with a cargo of Tyne coal, road-rail, pig-lead, firewood, iron-ware and cheap tin trays, butting through the Channel on its way to Marseilles and passing a dirty French coaster coming the other way with near identical wares is producing real costs for doubtful ends, while the *environmental* costs of aircraft guzzling cheap non-renewable fuel as they speed through the heavens carrying mangoes to Sainsburys or carnations to the Riviera would, if they had to be met by the shipper, bring large sections of trade to a grinding halt.

Many countries have economic systems which are so divorced from reality and have such bad accounting methods that they are due for very ugly shocks anyway. It is not just that they are borrowing from the global commons that which they are unable to return. Some countries, like the US, with large national debts have already borrowed from the future more than they are likely to be able to repay in a sustainable world. Others have been more circumspect. Japan has bought relatively low unemployment with a high cost of living and little consumer credit, a bargain which it was right for them to make (and which it would be right for us to make).

The payment of true costs by society would bring many living standards in the developed world tumbling down. How much *real* wealth do we produce? The truth is that just as when we were a colonial power we became prosperous on the lifeblood of our colonies, while persuading ourselves that we were leading the heathen from darkness to light, so our post-colonial regime with its huge ecological footprint[15] extending into the Third World is, with almost equally horrific self-righteousness, sucking the blood of other nations in order that we may gorge ourselves (or more likely save ourselves from pernicious anaemia) — and it is finding that the blood-sucking is becoming more difficult, because of the free movement of capital to areas where the TNCs can use it more profitably.

And travel itself, let alone trade, can be a menace. It has long been known that the diseases of 'civilised' people can do more than decimate unprepared native tribes. But now we are in a situation where a new virus can board a plane and travel several thousand miles in a day.[16]

The need for a new kind of economics

You have to be blind not to see that the structure of power in both of the traditional systems — worse in the socialist systems, but in all of the advanced capitalist systems — is such that they generate outcome results that are not compatible with ecological sustainability.

Gar Alperovitz (President of the National Centre for Economic and Security Alternatives)

But all is not lost. The new ecological economics which is coming will certainly involve control of capital movements so that what nations justly make and earn they may be able to keep. (And as a first step towards that, we will have to work out new methods of accounting; for as a study of the US Current Account shows, the whole matter of calculating international finance is in question. How much cross-border trading actually takes place within individual firms?)[17]

And we will have to control how the necessary investment is deployed. Because as the economic system works at the moment, 'if sufficient investment is not forthcoming today, unemployment will be here today. But if enough is invested today, still more will be needed tomorrow'.[18] In other words, in post-Keynesian economics, major growth of GNP is necessary to maintain full employment. But since infinite growth of GNP is a logical and practical impossibility, if we wish to keep full employment, or even provide everyone with worthwhile work (a different matter), we will have to look for a different system of economics.

The basis of the new economics is the realisation that there are four factors to be taken into account, not the old three of land, labour and capital. The four are ecological capital, human capital, social capital and manufactured capital.[19]

And four suggestions for the World Bank by Herman Daly are:

(1) stop counting the consumption of natural capital as income;

(2) tax labour and income less and throughput more;

(3) increase the productivity of natural capital (investment should be the limiting factor, and to the extent that natural capital has replaced human-made capital as the limiting factor, the investment focus should shift correspondingly);

4) decrease international trade.

Dealing with wastes

'Practically nowhere on this earth are signs of the human economy absent. From the centre of Antarctica to the top of Mount Everest, human wastes are obvious and increasing'.[20] (And incidentally at these extremes with their low temperatures human shit is quite literally there to stay!)

Plenty produces, eventually or not so eventually, what we call rubbish and rubbish has got to be disposed of, but the disposal causes problems. For centuries we have been able to use the common property of the world, such as the atmosphere and the sea, to receive our discards virtually without cost. But now we have reached a stage where air is becoming too polluted for human and other health and the pollution of the sea is killing the fish. Private ownership and private use in a competitive market gives rise to Adam Smith's 'invisible hand' which operates beneficially for the common good — but Herman Daly points out that public ownership with unrestrained private use gives rise to an invisible foot which kicks the common good to pieces.[21]

After all, there is not much point increasing human wealth by manufacturing things which people need or at any rate are prepared to buy, if human wealth is simultaneously decreased by the expenditures needed to get rid of the detritus arising from such manufacture.

Land-fill sites are becoming harder to find; ordinary garbage is shipped even further or needs greater expenditure to dispose of while specialised chemical or nuclear waste is clearly even more of a problem. (Quite apart from the fact that we have not faced up to the problem of how we dispose of our nuclear power stations when they have finished their comparatively short useful life — if any).

Dumps we used to regard quite responsibly as suitable for waste have proved not to be so; persistent toxic chemicals such as DDT and heavy metal compounds have already spread throughout the marine ecosystem. And spreading in this context does not just mean dilution, as the chemicals and metals accumulate in living organisms and make fish inedible as well as sick.

Water, earth and air are all becoming overloaded; an entire generation of Mexico City children may have been intellectually stunted by lead-poisoning and, as I have already pointed out, we are not feeling very well ourselves.

Global warming (if it is happening, and the evidence, including the dramatic diminution of the Antarctic ice sheets, appears to be growing ever stronger that it is) is going to produce many more problems.

The tragedies are building up everywhere and it is important not just to aggregate them but to look at them in reasonable bite-sizes (or byte-sizes?) which our minds can accommodate.

So Thomas Berry [22] points out that 'The Philippines, at the beginning of this century, had six million people. That figure has doubled every twenty years, from six to twelve, twelve to twenty-four, twenty-four to fifty. The number is 70 million now and that is in the process of doubling. There will be over 100 million people shortly after the year 2010. Meanwhile their mangrove swamps are destroyed, and eighty per cent of the coral reefs which are among the richest ecosystems on the planet, themselves providing a valuable sink for atmospheric gases, are severely damaged. A third of the soil is severely damaged, two-thirds is partly damaged, and the rainforest that once covered over 90% of the area will, it seems, soon be totally gone. Only 10% survives now.

So we can list disaster after disaster to the natural environment, all occurring in the process of what is ostensibly a better provision for people's needs. Why do they blast the fisheries? To feed people more efficiently. Why do they destroy the mangrove swamps? For the same reason. And where is it all going to end? In the impoverishment and death of millions of people. But as we look at various individual cases we can also learn to draw up tables by which we can compare them. For instance Pearce (in *Sustainable Development*), looking at Amazonian rainforest deforestation, lists as losses:

(1) loss of genetic material
(2) decline of unique ecosystems
(3) loss of population and disruption of culture
(4) spread of endemic diseases and pests
(5) loss of soil productivity
(6) long-term damage to regional climate (affecting neighbours)
(7) long-term damage to world climate patterns

Preventing loss of soil productivity

Although the loss of soil productivity on a major scale is something we shall look at later when we consider how to conduct sustainable agriculture, this is, I think, the right chapter in which to note one or two of the problems caused by intensive agriculture. These are many and include the problems of genetic engineering and the use of hormone 'therapy' to increase productivity.

In the *Times* recently the Medical Briefing reported that no group of people needs hormone replacement therapy more than agricultural workers, who have low levels of blood testosterone owing to the past use of hormones in animal husbandry, and that while these were now banned in Britain there was a move afoot to withdraw the ban.[21]

The destructiveness of war

There may well be those who think that war is far too important to be merely a sub-heading in a chapter, even one on the cancer of capitalism; but destructive though it is, it is not of a different order to soil degradation as a threat to man on the planet.

Indeed there are those who argue that war is not necessarily a disaster in the present situation. Those who look at the demoralisation of modern male youth recall with something approaching nostalgia that war is a traditional way of channelling the aggression of the young. And it is also mooted as a method (although admittedly a not very adequate one) of reducing world population.

But while many people, including Mr Jorrocks,[22] have sought substitutes for war, there is near universal agreement that war destroys too many resources and that although it may be impossible to abolish altogether, nevertheless in a sustainable world it must be controlled.

And this means stringent control of arms. It is of course part of the basic defence mechanism of capitalism that trade is ethically neutral. 'If I sell gas ovens to Nazi Germany, it is no business of mine what they do with them. If I don't provide them, someone else will.' In fact we know that this is nonsense when we take it to its logical conclusion. In Britain at any rate we do not regard the peddling of heroin as morally neutral. And a situation such as occurred in Britain in 1994/5, whereby at the same time aid to the Third World was cut and provision of money for an export guarantee scheme for arms was quintupled, is morally unacceptable to most people.

1   Wendell Berry: 'Sales Resistance' (*Resurgence* 165).
2   Arthur Lubow: 'The Vodka Has Legs' (*New Yorker* 12/9/94).
3   Deep in our collective mythology (and of enormous importance) lies the Grail legend in which a good knight perpetuates chaos in the world by not asking the right question.
4   Deuteronomy 30.19-20.
5   Joel Kurtzman: *The Death of Money* (Simon & Schuster 1993).
6   *The Times* (20/4/96).
7   'The End of Nations' (*The Times* 31/8/95).
8   *On the Principles of Political Economy and Taxation* (Penguin p155).
9   UNRISD: *States of Disarray.*
10 Chesterton: *On Love.*
11 James Goldsmith: *The Response* (pp18 &19).
12 *The Immigration Dilemma* p83.

13   John Ruskin: *Essays on Political Economy: Maintenance of Life*.
14   Anatole Karetsky in *The Times* of 2/11/95.
15   Ecological footprints have been defined 'as the aggregate area of land and water in various ecological categories that is claimed by participants in an economy to produce all the resources they consume, and to absorb the wastes they generate on a continuous basis, using prevailing technology'. This comes from an extremely important article by Mathis Wackernagel & William E. Rees in EE 20/1.
16   Professor Jonathan Mann in the preface to Laurie Garrett's *The Coming Plague*.
17   Obie Wichard & Jeffrey Lowe: *An owner-based Disaggregation of the US Current Account* (Survey of Current Business 10/95, Bureau of Economic Analysis, Washington).
18   Evesy Domar quoted in Daly (1).
19   *Wealth beyond Measure* by Paul Ekins, Mayer Hillman & Robert Hutchison.
20   Robert Goodland: 'The case that the World has reached Limits' in Ch 2 of *Population, Technology & Lifestyle*.
21   Herman E. Daly: *Valuing the Earth*.
22   Thomas Berry CP (with Thomas Clarke C.J.): *Befriending the Earth* (Twenty Third Publications: Mystic Connecticut).
21   'Medical Briefing' in *The Times* (14/10/95).
22   'Hunting is the image of war without its guilt, and only five and twenty per cent of its danger' (*Handley Cross* by R.S. Surtees).

Chapter 3

Sighting the abyss: the first efforts to halt the slide

Towards what ultimate point is society tending by its industrial progress?
When the progress ceases, in what condition are we to expect that it will
leave mankind?

John Stuart Mill

Along with a growing awareness that the yellow brick road to the
Emerald City appears to be petering out into an illkept criminal-
haunted byway, there has come the sudden realisation on the part of the
world's leaders of the finitude of life on our planet.

Twenty years ago hardly anyone would have forecast that in the very near
future there would be an international summit meeting dedicated to the examination of that issue; let alone that it would result in near unanimous
agreement that there was a threat to the planet so serious that it had to be met
by international action so far ranging in its implications that it would involve
a revolution in political and economic thinking. But the increasing pressure
of immediate practical problems, together with the thinking and publications
of a number of far-sighted people, largely from the academic world (although
often on what had heretofore been its fringes), did trigger the Rio Conference
of 1992. And, partly as a result of that conference, it may be possible for us
to find a path to civilisation other than the yellow brick road, even if that civilisation proves not even to resemble an Emerald City.

A planet with a full-repairing lease

So we are catapulted in the course of one generation from the belief that we
have full mastery and ownership of this planet to a realisation that all we have
got is a full repairing lease. Now, anyone who has occupied a house with a full
repairing lease will know that it is a restricter of freedom, an expensive burden
and a stimulus to thrifty thinking. You cannot knock down an ugly outhouse
or build on an attic extension and you have perpetually to be putting money
by for the moment when you have to hand the property back in the state in

which you received it. Whether the landlord of the planet is seen as God, Gaia or our great-grandchildren we can be sure that if we do not fulfil the terms of the lease we or our heirs face the severest penalties.

Economics as a subset of ecology

In effect the result of coming to terms with these truths is the realisation that, as we have already seen, the science of economics is basically a subset of ecology.[1]

Persuaded by those imprisoned within the discipline of economics, and receiving approval from those who gained in financial terms from the belief, the world had thought that the realm of economics was a self-governing discipline subject to laws which were clearly abstractions from the real world and therefore not to be questioned except occasionally by the inner circle for the purpose of fine tuning. But the world is slowly now beginning to realise that economics is merely a tool to be employed, as selectively as any other tool, in global housekeeping, much as double-entry can be employed in domestic housekeeping. And our full repairing lease on the planet means that we must only use the tool in ways which contribute to the planet's preservation.

This means that market forces can no longer be regarded as an 'invisible hand' which will put everything right. It is also the 'invisible foot' which sends the household gods — very often, following sod's law, the most precious ones — crashing to the floor.

Society in control of market mechanisms

Only if society acts collectively to influence and constrain individual market decisions can sustainability be achieved. This does not mean the use of vulgar force to twist people's behaviour into forms they do not want. On the contrary a process of education accompanied by a lavish supply of the right kind of carrot and a mild application of constraint should be enough. For this is not a new kind of ideology to be imposed; it is the innate wisdom of the human race to be tapped.

And this must be done collectively because we are not capable of doing it individually. In the words of Lord Lindsay of Birker:

> I am unjust but I can strive for justice.
>   My life's unkind but I can vote for kindness.
> I, the unloving, say life should be lovely;
>   I, that am blind, cry out against my blindness.
>
> Come, let us vote against our human nature,
>   Crying to God in all the polling places
> To heal our everlasting sinfulness,
>   And make us sages with transfigured faces.[2]

Except that I maintain we will be voting with and not against at least a major part, and that the most basic, of our human nature.

Very often, far from acting in a revolutionary manner, all we are doing is enabling ourselves collectively to obey the 'laws' of economics more thoroughly by, for instance, forcing firms and consumers to bear the full costs of their activities either through regulation or taxation.[3]

A new category: existence values

But we may have to expand the repertoire of economics somewhat. For instance ecological economists have more and more come to recognise the importance of 'existence value'. It is more or less impossible without descending into cloud-cuckoo land or obscenity to work out the 'economic values' of a landscape or a species of birds. Many earnest economists try to do so and their efforts may produce useful subsidiary arguments for conservation, but no normal person can read their efforts (always assuming that they are legible and not hopelessly peppered with equations) without bursting into either tears or helpless mirth.

We all do know that our lives would be poorer without Mount Everest or tigers in the wild, even if we have never seen either with our own eyes. That is what is meant by existence value and the fact that it is not capable of being squeezed into equations is not the least of the guarantees of its importance.

And existence value is not only applicable to nature. The same difficulty in valuation applies to the existence of quality arts. You can do endless economic sums as to why it is more important to put Bruce Forsyth on TV than Grand Opera but even most of those who never watch opera know that it is important that it is screened. They set an unquantifiable, but nonetheless real, value on the existence of high culture.

The husbandry of non-renewable resources

The idea of a full repairing lease on the planet immediately suggests some basic rules, such as that if we do not treasure our non-renewable resources then we (the planet) will be in trouble. It is true that in many fields there seems to be no immediate need for panic. Turner, Pearce and Bateman conclude that 'Overall, although the management of resource scarcity is a far from straightforward task and the published results of the various "economic" scarcity studies are not consistent, it is not likely that the world is suddenly going to run short of the minerals and fuels it needs for future economic developments.'[4]

There are of course those who say that classical economics, even if regarded only as a tool, does provide the answer and that when one source eventually becomes too scarce and therefore too expensive we merely switch by the natural operation of the market to that substitute which has by then become comparatively cheaper.

In many instances those who argue this way are doing all their costings in purely monetary terms and ignoring the fact that the source which the market will substitute will already be more expensive in the true global currency of energy.

But even if we do not make an elementary mistake in our calculations about substitutes we will be ignoring the long-term logic which should quickly remind us that we are embarking on a long march through different non-renewable commodities, each one by definition more expensive than the last, till we reach the inevitable safety of the renewables, on which we then have perforce to rely without any interim help from the non-renewables. Far better, surely, to move slowly forward using the non-renewables sparingly as we learn to adapt to our new way of life.

All our experience seems to show that when there is no immediate need to panic, no one does anything at all until it is too late, but we may expect that in the course of dealing with those problems where there does appear to be something approaching a need to panic, we may learn habits of mind and a new way of living which will lead us to use non-renewables sparingly.

Population, entropy and sinks

What are these panic station problems? Most obvious and most fundamental is a growing world population and the need to feed it. Close on its heels is the slightly more debatable but no less real problem of the global 'sinks', those areas such as the oceans and the atmosphere where we reckon to dispose of the detritus of our civilisation and which are getting rapidly more and more clogged. And since nature is remarkably economical and the same medium often (if not always) doubles as both a source and a sink we will find, say, that increasing use of the sea as a sink makes it decreasingly useful as a source. The more radioactive materials you put into it, the fewer edible herrings you will fish out of it.

But if sinks and sources are both producing problems of scarcity, that scarcity is in the last resort backed up by the ultimate shortage, that of free available energy, governed by the law of entropy.

Entropy, which appears to be a peculiarly elusive concept, has been defined as 'a measure of the unavailable energy in a thermodynamic system'. We are permanently in the process of trying to turn relatively free energy, say in oil and steel, via the manufacture of goods such as cars into the totally irretrievable energy which results when the car is put on the scrap heap. (Admittedly you can reclaim from the scrap heap but each time you do this you dissipate available energy.) So industry is permanently dissipating available energy and moving matter from a low entropy to a high entropy state. Some energy is so free that it will be available for as long, say, as the sun exists but there is a great deal of semi-available energy which we are dissipating all the time. And that is another reason to add to those which we will find in Chapter 5 for investing in low-technology goods rather than high-technology ones.[5]

Population

But a more urgent and fundamental, because more massive and intractable, problem is that of population. Until Thomas Malthus focused at the beginning of the eighteenth century on the natural tendency of the population to increase faster than the means of subsistence, it is probably true to say that there had been little reason for the opinion forming classes to consider the problems this raised. This was partly because one of the stories in the Bible recounts that when the world was fairly empty of people God had issued a commandment to 'be fruitful and multiply', partly because humankind in its arrogance believed that 'you cannot have too much of a good thing', partly because of natural instincts, and partly because resources did not *appear* to be limited. There were still vast areas of the world virtually undiscovered and the means to make them productive through improved technology was already getting into its stride.[6]

The spectre of over-population raised by Malthus was dismissed as all early warnings are apt to be (cf. *Limits to Growth*, below) because it was seen not to have taken various factors into account. There were enough of these to enable the sceptics to ignore the basic truth at the centre of his argument. But the subject of the finitude of the world and the problems of increasing population had been put on the agenda of opinion formers and were unlikely to be removed. In time it gave rise to the school of science fiction which solves the problem by having humans colonise the stars and it possibly even influenced those who poured vast sums of money into the space programme, instead of solving the more urgent but apparently less tractable problems of the human race at home.

The publication of *Limits to Growth* by the Club of Rome in 1972 was a touchpaper for the modern great debate on the subject and it was closely followed by a shift from the idea that resources would not prove enough for an expanding population to the additional and complementary notion that the mechanisms for dealing with the detritus of prosperity, such as the emissions from fossil fuel, would equally not prove adequate.

A strong rearguard action then set itself to prove, often highly successfully, that the so-called doomsters were wrong in detail and went on to imply that therefore the whole pessimistic scenario could be ignored.

Often it was assertions rather than arguments which both sides deployed but when it was the latter the arguments of the optimists appeared to revolve round the assumption that while physical resources might indeed be finite, the ingenuity of the human mind was not — and that therefore we need the maximum number of people in order that they may think of methods to deploy the finite resources better.[7] This argument clearly has some logical validity even though it smacks slightly of setting monkeys to work with typewriters in order that they may produce the complete works of Shakespeare.

The increase of world resource and sink problems is such that while the doomsters are continually failing to clinch their points and their detailed forecasts prove fallible, the ranks of those who find it possible to maintain the main tenet of the 'resource optimists'[8] — which is that somehow science will solve the many problems and the world can continue on in the same old way — are being steadily diminished. So much so that by the time the UNCED (United Nations Conference on Environment and Development) Rio Conference of 1992 was held not a single country, not even the United States,[9] was prepared to dissent from the proposition that the world must adopt a 'sustainable economy' if the future of humans on the planet is to be ensured.

It should be emphasised that the most urgent fear is not that there will be widespread famine, though such an eventuality should not be ruled out if present trends of population growth, pollution, international trade and wealth distribution persist, while possible climate changes raise further worrying issues. Nor is shortage of water seen as the most urgent problem, although according to Sandra Postel of the Worldwatch Institute[10] per capita fresh water supplies will drop by more than a third by 2025. The most immediately vulnerable sector appears to be the sink potential of the planet, for our ability to cope with our own excreta in all its forms is proving increasingly inadequate.

As I write these words in London, Government ministers are issuing warnings against bringing out our cars to add to the already disease-, if not death-, dealing state of the atmosphere. By the time that this book is published that will probably be seen as a minor incident, even though it would have been dismissed by many as incredible if it had been forecast even ten years ago.

The real fear is that the pressure of population on sources and sinks combined will lead to a number of global developments which together will pose problems of war, of migration, of resulting disease and of economic breakdown with which we will not be able to cope.

However the only way in which we might be able to cope with all this is not by standing still and digging in, a process in any case where over-populated England is bound to be a loser and where the only possible winners could be islands such as St Helena, isolated, ringed with unscalable cliffs and with a terrain not productive enough to tempt outsiders but just barely fertile enough to feed the population.

The only hope is to move forward to a different organisation of the world in which growth is seldom quantitative and change is achieved within a framework of compassion and with a profound understanding of the interconnectedness of all phenomena. Indeed, we need to stop referring to *growth* as an objective and instead seek *development*, making sure that we understand that the development is qualitative rather than quantitative. 'Development', says Herman Daly, 'means the qualitative improvement in the structure, design and composition of the physical stocks of wealth that results from greater knowledge, both of technique and of purpose'.[11]

This move will need great sensitivity, and nowhere will this sensitivity be more needed than in the tricky area of population policy. There can be no doubt that of all the ecological problems which beset us population is the most fundamental. It is pressure of people that causes not only the 'source' but also the 'sink' problems.

And one of those sink problems is the rise of enormous conurbations, such as Calcutta and Mexico City, not to mention London and New York. This is inevitable since even if the world decides (as I hope it will) to go for a new-style people-intensive rural economy, there is a definite limit to the carrying capacity of the countryside, and every surplus consuming unit (commonly called a baby) which appears must by definition go to swell the numbers in what I suppose we must euphemistically call the towns, but which are in reality more and more becoming glorified sink repositories for humans..

It is worth noting in passing that it is clear that larger conurbations need higher taxes which gives force even in classical economic terms to the rather old-fashioned ideal of an optimal population meeting the carrying capacity of a given area of land. But the main pressure to revive that ideal comes from the relative scarcity of natural resources (counting the ability to provide adequate sinks as a resource, which it is).

In a world in which we are striving for sustainable development we should adopt Virginia Abernethy's definition of carrying capacity: 'the number of individuals who can be supported without degrading the physical, cultural and social environment; that is, without reducing the ability of the environment to sustain the desired quality of life over the long term'.[12]

Admittedly the equation of what size population can be carried is complicated by the existence of the rich who cause disproportionate damage to their environment, but the problems of the human race will not be solved by the methods of the late Revd Marcus Morris, himself a rich man through achievement, who once suggested to me at least semi-seriously that the answer to most of our problems was to put all the rich up against a wall and shoot them. (Presumably, for at least two reasons, that of capacity and that of ideology, the Great Wall of China was the one he had in mind!) And, talking of China, we need to find some less coercive method than either Marcus Morris's, attractive though that may sometimes seem to us, or that of China itself. (And, since rich is a purely comparative term, you cannot get rid of the rich by merely shooting one generation of them. In order to abolish the rich, you must make all people wealthy!)

The trouble is that there is some urgency. The trends of population size are still pointing upward and a lot of hard work must be done quickly if we are to cause them to level out — which is the necessary first step before we can move to making the decline. Some recent forecasts[13] suggest that, assuming a massive transfer of economic resources from industrialised to developing countries and equally massive direct aid to family planning (and that is quite an assumption), the global population might level out at about 8,000 million by the year 2035 and decline to 6,000 million by 2070. The International Conference on Population and Development held in Cairo in 1994, however, set its sights rather more realistically on levelling out population at 9,800 million by 2050.

Such forecasts are now under challenge as a result of the AIDS epidemic. It is now thought by a number of experts that there will be no population growth in Sub-Saharan Africa over the next twenty years and that shortly after that there may be a similar situation in South East Asia and (probably) India. The position in China is obscure.

Nevertheless every country and every political movement must have policies designed to control population as well as AIDS. These should be embarked on now.

In terms which we can understand easily it appears that we are talking of achieving a reproduction rate of an average of less than two births per woman from now on (as opposed to a natural fertility rate of perhaps ten).

Zero population growth appears already to have been achieved in many Western countries (although US family size is creeping up from 1.9 children a few years ago to 2.1 now). The 'completed fertility' rates (by definition always some thirty years in arrears) of European countries were by 1958 under 2 for every country except France, which has a record of pro-natalist policies based on the proposition that there can never be too many French men and women in the world, Ireland, where the strong influence of the Roman Catholic Church and its control of the availability of contraceptives resisted the tendency of other Catholic countries to hear dogma but apply commonsense, and at least one of the Scandinavian countries. But by 1992 the annual tendency had sunk to under 2 for every country except Ireland and Sweden.[14]

And, as I have said, this is a matter of extreme urgency. Paul Harrison has pointed out[15] that we suffer from the Hamlet syndrome. In the play 'Hamlet knows from early on that he must kill his father's murderer Claudius. But before he makes up his mind to do so six innocent lives have been lost and Hamlet himself has only half an hour to live'. Harrison then goes on to summarise four achievable objectives which, if targeted firmly enough and started early enough, might just do the trick.

Those four objectives are: a high level of female education and literacy; a decent status for women, including the right to control and inherit property and to work outside the home for equal pay; a priority for mother and child health care to bring down levels of infant mortality; and easy access to a wide and free choice of family planning methods with good counselling and medical back-up.

These objectives, which with relatively minor reservations are widely accepted in principle by almost all except, in the case of the last one, by the hierarchy of the Roman Catholic Church, are nevertheless far from achievement. According to reliable resources, in Africa 77% of women who say that they do not want more children are without contraceptive provision, in Asia 57% and in Latin America 43%. The objectives therefore appear appallingly difficult to achieve.

However where such methods as Harrison suggests are applied, as in the Indian state of Kerala, very good results have been seen. Amartya Sen has pointed out that Kerala had a marginally higher birth rate than China in 1979 and by 1991 had one marginally lower, with no compulsion having been exercised at all. Kerala sank from having a fertility rate of 3.0 to one of 1.8 by means of 'widespread education, including female education, a tradition of property rights less biased against women than in most of Asia and widespread public discussion, particularly about the emancipation of women'.[16]

Female education and empowerment has the further contributory factor of adding wealth, or at least preventing its dissipation — for where women have a say money is less likely to be squandered on cigarettes and alcohol.[17]

And we can take some heart from the basic theory put forward by Professor Virginia Abernethy, which does not appear yet to have entered the thought stream of most of those who hover around the edges of population policy. (I use the word 'hover' advisedly because there seems to be an almost prudish unwillingness to tackle the problem head on.) Professor Abernethy's theory comes from examining what causes population surges and she claims that the trigger has usually been the opening up of some new opportunity, such as settled agriculture, which changes ideas of the future, offering a prospect either of hope or despair.

Such a belief may come from very different events, many of them seen as good in themselves. It may come from the shift from nomadic to settled life but it may also come from a belief that some or many of your children may emigrate.[18] And redistribution of land, foreign aid,[19] oil revenues and economic liberalisation have all proved triggers at some time and in some place.

That some process of adapting to carrying capacity has happened in the past, in the absence of the triggers of great fears and hopes, is undoubted, even if the mechanism of adaptation is not completely understood. The basic process seems to be that a whole culture has almost instinctively understood the constraints and reacted to them.

There are therefore obviously problems with cultures like the American one which is conditioned by the open frontier mentality. And equally obviously the stabilising process stands more chance of working in self-contained communities, of a comprehensible size, which is why a number of the examples of successful adaptation seem to be found in islands.

If the psychological processes of motivation are not fully understood, at least the mechanisms which have been used are a matter of record. Solutions have come through an emphasis on virginity before marriage coupled with late marriages, the marriage of poor men to older women,[20] the use of contraceptive and abortifacient devices or even infanticide. More modern (and much less unattractive) methods are the ones which we have already noted as efficacious in Kerala.

Lack of paid employment may (curiously) also sometimes be a deterrent to breeding. The birth rate in Western Europe (including Britain) in the nineties is declining and a European Union report suggests that this may be partly due to people being more interested in retraining for jobs than in having more babies. And this may come, my daughter suggests, from having been involved in responsible jobs before they 'retired to breed' and therefore wanting to return to a more or less equally interesting job.

A population policy for Britain

> You want a self-supporting country. We're parasites and must live by our exports, and that means capitalism until the time comes when we have halved our population and can be independent of our neighbours.
>
> Adam Melfort in *A Prince of the Captivity*, by John Buchan

> 'Who are the surplus people? Clearly it is not us, so it must be them.'

The UK needs, of course, to look at its own population size, even if it has ceased to grow, since by any rational sustainable standards we (mainly England) are very over-populated. Our footprint is far too large, even in terms of food supply. We have already looked at the ecological yardstick that no territory/nation should carry more people than it can feed and it is equally ecologically sound to carry this proposition one stage further and say that we ought to feed our own people for the most part locally and stop spending energy transporting large quantities of food about the world, sometimes from countries which are themselves starving. (It should not be forgotten that under our present economic system the Irish food famines of the last century happened while ships were leaving Irish ports loaded with cattle!)

Any population policy for the UK would revolve round:

(1) an improvement in educational standards for the whole population including the poorest;

(2) an improvement in health (including general welfare) standards for the whole population including the poorest; and

(3) an employment/training policy that allowed poor, under-educated and probably unemployed girls to find their identity without having to become pregnant.

We in the UK would find it very difficult to feed our population ourselves today. It could be done but the diet would be extremely monotonous. We could probably more or less feed ourselves if we were pushed to it. We are helped in this by the fact that we have had in the living memory of many of us exactly that experience. In the Second World War we got near to feeding ourselves although at one moment our food supplies were down to ten days needs. The figures for potential production (as opposed to what we actually do produce) today are not easily arrived at but if we said that by stretching every muscle and using a number of agricultural techniques which are almost certainly not sustainable in the long run and which are extremely bad for species diversity we could possibly just feed ourselves, although on a very dull diet (needing imported Spam or even Snoek to liven it up!), we would not be far wrong.

In a truly sustainable world, every nation needs to have an economic footprint no larger than itself. To adapt the words of R. H. Tawney[21] from a personal to an international level, a nation must not 'wear several men's clothes, occupy several men's dinners, occupy several families' houses and live several men's lives'. That means that it must not only be able to feed itself but to a large extent actually do so, matching the import of those foodstuffs which it cannot for climatic reasons produce itself with exports of other foodstuffs wanted by other countries. If we are to achieve this there will in practice have to be a major population decline, with all the problems for the demographic profile that that involves. All that is so if we treat the UK as the relevant unit which must feed itself. The agricultural capacity for England, the UK and the EU is as follows:

England	0.19 hectares (of agricultural land) per person
UK	0.29 hectares (of agricultural land) per person
EU	2.85 hectares (of agricultural land) per person

We could therefore ride on the back of the European Union rather than face the difficulties of demographic structure caused by reduction of the population of England. (As a person who feels his roots primarily in European Christendom rather than in pre-Norman Britain I have a personal bias towards this!)

But such an assumption rests on the EU holding together and the world abandoning any attempt to administer a GATT in agricultural products. There are reasons to believe (see *The Great Reckoning* by Davidson and Rees-Mogg) that the latter may be going to happen anyway.

GATT must become GAST (a General Agreement on Sustainable Trade) and to that end nations should be encouraged to:

(1) restrict the export of scarce resources where they are not managed sustainably and

(2) stop the export of any product (e.g. harmful pesticides) which are banned in the exporting country

There are other desirable ecological policies which are not essential to a proposed population policy but which fall into the same area of reform.

For instance there is an ecologically unsound settlement pattern almost everywhere in the world but certainly in England and Scotland (Wales on the other hand is a model of what should be). The development pattern of cities fed by their surrounding countryside becomes impossible as the cities grow. There is a revealing moment in the history of the London Boroughs, early in the nineteenth century, when they ceased to be paid by contractors for the privilege of removing the rubbish and instead had to pay the contractors. This was probably the moment of collapse of a healthy symbiosis between town and country. Given the appalling permanent damage that building does to the land, this elephantiasis of urban development becomes almost impossible to reverse (cf the difficulty of returning wartime airfields to agricultural land).

And a corollary of treating the EU as the basic agriculturally self-sufficient unit is that we would then be able to adopt low instead of high farming, abandon setaside, reduce the size of our farms and stop giving over good land to golf courses and motorways. This would of course be very expensive in traditional economic terms but the choice may be between being paupers in a totally unhealthy society and economy and being paupers in a healthy one.

The steps on the way to population limitation and eventual decline of course include emphasis on the right kind of sex education, a popular campaign of population awareness, and immigration and emigration numbers at the very least in balance.

What is needed above all is awareness. It is my firm belief that democracy works (when people are not treated as mushrooms: kept in the dark and fed on horseshit). But there is a horrible story of the Fifth Horseman of the

Apocalypse who rode ahead of the other four (War, Famine, Pestilence and Death) warning the world of their coming. But the people would not listen. And when the Four had done their work and the Fifth Horseman rode back over the devastation, the few survivors reviled him: 'You did not warn us enough. You should have made us listen!'[22]

To be taking population policy seriously, not just for 'the world' but for Britain would be a massive step forward. (No British political party except for the so-far ill-fated Ecology (Green) Party has even acknowledged that there is a need for one except in distant parts of the world.)

The inadequacy of sinks

(1) The atmosphere

But to return to the global scene: the second most urgent problem, after population, is that of dealing with the wastes of the industrial world (and the growing shortage of sinks to receive them). We have for far too long not minded what we have been pumping into the air and the sea. It is not that in Britain we have not noticed. Edward I set up a commission to defuse Londoners' anger about pollution from burning coal. It sat for 25 years without achieving anything. Six hundred years later the metropolis was still famous for its 'London Particular' fogs named not for their content of particulates but for their resemblance in colour to a popular blend of Madeira wine. And in 1952 the Great Smog lasted for four days accelerating the deaths of 4,000 people.

That time we passed the Clean Air Act, only to find in the last forty years that there are as many demons just as bad though not so obvious in the bright sunlight; lead from petrol affecting our children's brains, ozone and nitrogen dioxide from cars, and sulphur dioxide from power stations.

These are the great blankets of filth, often not visible, emanating from the richer cities of the world and they were even a source of pride to some. 'See our smoke?' said Josiah Bounderby in Dickens' *Hard Times*, 'That's meat and drink to us. It is the healthiest thing in the world to us, especially for the lungs.' He would not abate the pollution in his factories for 'all the humbugging sentiment in Great Britain and Ireland'. And although Dickens was as usual being heavily satirical it would almost certainly not have been impossible to find real life Bounderbys. Indeed you can find them today, those people who oppose environmentalism if it seems to threaten jobs in the short term.

We know how to deal with these problems, but most of the solutions are tied in with difficult political (as well as complex technical) decisions such as tackling the problem of the enormous use of private cars. For instance, a vital first step is to avoid critical loads of pollution, defined as the level of deposition below which, according to current scientific knowledge, no damage to sensitive ecosystems will occur. This is the strong, and therefore the expensive, solution, as opposed to the one which industry and the Exchequer prefer, which is a cost-benefit policy, weighing (e.g.) the loss of species against the money to be expended.

(2) The oceans

Although we continue to pollute the atmosphere we probably do more lasting harm to the oceans which we have long treated as our waste-disposal units of last resort. 'That is the proper place for the rubbish,' we say. 'Isn't nature/technology wonderful?' Well, yes it is — but not that wonderful. Most of the coastal fisheries of the industrial countries of the world have been ruined by our detritus. 'Off the Palos Verdes peninsula just South of Los Angeles, a city sewage plant covered an 8km sq kelp forest (home of fish and the food of fish) with toxin-laden and heavy metal-laced sludge in a mere 40 years. It is a combination of this pollution with over-fishing which has brought us to the point where the Food and Agriculture Organisation of the UN estimates that all 17 of the world's major fishing areas have either reached or exceeded their natural limits.[23]

1   *The Journal of Ecological Economics* 15/1.
2   I have been unable to track down the exact reference for these verses which I copied into my Commonplace Book a long time ago. If any reader could supply me with the the full text I would be most grateful.
3   Part of this last section, as of others later on dealing with the cohesion of society, is taken, sometimes verbally, from the admirable pamphlet *Sustainability and Socialism* by Michael Jacobs, published by SERA (the Socialist Environment and Resources Association).
4   R. Kerry Turner, David Pearce & Ian Bateman: *Environmental Economics,* p234.
5   For a much fuller and more satisfactory account of the problems posed by the laws relating to entropy, see the work of Nicholas Georgescu-Roegen and especially his chapter 'The Entropy Law and the Economic Problem' in Daly and Townsend: *Valuing the Earth.*
6   As farsighted a thinker as John Ruskin dismissed the idea that there was any danger of over-population for those reasons.
7   E.g. Peter (Lord) Bauer: 'World Numbers will look after Themselves' (*The Times* 31/08/95).
8   The resource optimists can refer their opponents to the findings in *Blueprint 3* (Pearce et al), that most resources (including petroleum, natural gas, aluminium, gold, silver, zinc, coal and copper) show no signs of increasing scarcity. On the other hand there is no doubt at all about there being a heavy rate of species extinction (1-5% per decade).
9   The US will almost certainly be the natural last-ditch protagonist of growth', partly because it is always galling for a power which regards itself with some, though decreasing, justification as the most powerful in the world to recognise that its power has limits, and partly because its whole history is governed by the largely valid myth of the expanding frontier, reinforced by having finally moved the frontier outward by putting men on the moon.
10   Sandra Postel in *People and The Planet*, Vol 2 No 2.
11   Herman Daly in 'Boundless Bull' (*Resurgence* 1750)

12   Virginia Abernethy: *Population Politics*.

13   S. E. Jorgensen in *Ecological Economics*, Vol 11, No 1.

14   The source of these rather complicated figures is *The Eurostat Yearbook 1995*.

15   Paul Harrison: *The Third Revolution*.

16   Amartya Sen: 'Wrongs and Rights in Development' in *Prospect*, Oct 95.

17   UNDP Human Development 96.

18   A. W. Brittain: 'Anticipated Child loss to Migration and Sustained High Fertility in an East Caribbean population' in *Social Biology* 38 (1991) and D. Friedlander: 'Demographic Responses and Socioeconomic Structure: Population Processes in England and Wales in the Nineteenth Century,' in *Demography* 20 (1983).

19   Realisation of this suggests that the channelling of foreign aid into population control measures needs to be accompanied by discrimination and even restraint in provision of other aid. The need also for tact in such situations hardly needs to be emphasised. See John Wyon and J.E. Gordon: *The Khanna Study: Population Problems in the Rural Punjab* (Cambridge: Harvard University Press). But the provision of microloans to small ventures, which appears to be a growing trend, probably avoids the danger.

20   B. S. Low and A. L. Clarke: 'Resources and the Life Course: Patterns in the Demographic Transition' in *Ethology & Sociobiology*, 13 (1992).

21   R. H. Tawney: *The Acquisitive Society*.

22   G. Edwards in *Power Magazine*, Jan 1945; a story paralleled by that told by Jesus of Nazareth about Dives and Lazarus.

23   For a thorough and spine-chilling account of the state of the oceans, see the comprehensively documented Worldwatch Paper 116 *Reversing the Decline of the Oceans*, by Peter Webber (Worldwatch Institute 11/93).

Chapter 4

Glimpsing the far side: what is wealth?

Among the ancients we discover no single enquiry as to what form of landed property etc is the most productive, which creates maximum wealth. The enquiry is always about what kind of property creates the best citizens.

Karl Marx

The Threshold hypothesis: for every society there seems to be a period in which economic growth [as conventionally measured] brings about an improvement in the quality of life but only up to a point — the threshold point — beyond which, if there is more economic growth, quality of life may begin to deteriorate. At that point quantitative growth must be metamorphosed into qualitative development.

Manfred Max-Neef

IT IS IMPORTANT at this stage of the book to have a quick look at how we can assess wealth. We have already seen from John Ruskin's definitions that wealth is not the same as riches or money. Riches is that which makes you rich and being rich is a comparative term, implying poverty in others; money is merely the vehicle in which riches (and sometimes wealth) can be stored and conveyed.

Wealth is wealth regardless of what other people may have and I can be wealthy without other people being poor. Wealth implies wellbeing and no society can be wealthy which has 'loadsamoney' in the bank balances of the rich but also unemployment and life on the modern equivalent of the bread-line for 25% of the population.

That is not to say that wealth is the good we ultimately seek, whatever that may be for each one of us. Wealth merely is the prerequisite for that degree of security, food and equipment we need in order to embark on the search for our particular Good. That is why religious who have taken a vow of poverty can nonetheless be wealthy.

Measuring wealth

There are various official measurements of wealth (or riches since the authorities do not yet differentiate between the two). Unfortunately the one which is most often used in measuring the riches of society is appallingly defective. But that fact, and the fact that everyone knows that fact, does not stop us from continuing to use it, since it is the one which best suits both classical economists and corporations.

That inadequate measurement is Gross National Product (GNP) and its variant, Gross Domestic Product (GDP). The difference between the two is that GNP includes income from overseas investment but excludes money earned by foreign companies from investment in this country. We will use the former in our discussions if only because GDP overstates the wealth of exploited countries by crediting to them the produce of their resources even if the full economic yield is being enjoyed by investors elsewhere.

If you want to raise Gross National Product (and all unthinking politicians do), here is a simple method. Get into your car and drive up the motorway, causing as many accidents as you can. The boost that that will give to the automobile manufacturing, repair and insurance industries and the use of hospitals and mortuaries will be both significant and valued as such. This is in spite of the fact that authorities in this country have worked out the financial cost of a traffic incident resulting in an injury other than death as £40,000.[1]

And even on the more positive side, what is thought to be gain is often not so in real terms. In 1989 Richard Douthwaite studied the results of the previous twenty-odd years of growth in the British economy, which as forecast by Rab Butler in 1954 had doubled the national per capita income. What he found was that 'the new wealth had been squandered on producing pallets and corrugated cardboard, non-returnable bottles and ring-pull drink cans. It had built airports, supertankers and heavy goods lorries, motorways, flyovers and [multi-storey] carparks'. It had put 2 million workers into the financial world, from which they were to be expelled in the nineties, and 3 million workers on the dole.[2]

On the other hand, the undoubted benefits in the health and welfare of the working classes (using that term in its widest sense) that could be seen in Britain at the end of the Second World War, in spite of the terrible financial crises which were to be felt in the aftermath, had come from 'a high demand for labor, the erosion of wage differentials, government control of profits and the implementation of a highly progressive tax structure'.[3]

The first fault in GNP, as you can tell from the above example, is that costs which are borne by the environment or by society and are not considered capable of being expressed in monetary terms are not deducted from the total, but actually contribute to it (e.g. in the wages of the undertakers!).

The second fault is that depletion of natural, as opposed to monetary, capital figures nowhere in the accounts. If you use up a mahogany forest (or more likely destroy a whole diversified forest in the quest for a few mahogany trees), that depletion appears nowhere in the sums, whereas the increased price of mahogany arising from the subsequent mahogany shortage does.

The third fault is that if you make do and mend or use secondhand goods, these wealth-saving activities do not register in the credit side of the balance-sheet — whereas if you put your broken goods out for the dustman to cart away and buy new ones, the latter purchases of course *do* register (as do the wages of the dustman and the diesel used by his lorry), thus ensuring unnecessary consumption of resources.

Fourth, actions to clean up disasters, as in our motorway example, register as positive goods, regardless of the fact that the disasters might have been prevented in the first place. And money spent on addictions counts equally with money spent on cures.

There are other faults, too, such as the inability to count non-consumptive leisure as a good; 'What is this life, if full of care, we have no time to stand and stare?'

The sum of these faults means that 'since GNP adds costs and benefits together instead of comparing them at the margin, we have no macro-level accounting by which an optimal scale could be identified... because:

(1) we fail to distinguish quantitative growth from qualitative development [see Chapter 2] and we classify all expansion as 'economic growth' without even recognising the possibility of 'anti-economic growth' — i.e. growth that costs us more than it is worth at the margin;

(2) we refuse to fight poverty by redistribution and sharing, or by controlling our own numbers, leaving 'economic growth' as the only acceptable cure for poverty. But once we are beyond the optimal scale, and growth makes us poorer rather than richer, even that reason becomes absurd.'[4]

For example, since the 1970s Indonesia has been a success story in the world press, achieving an exceptional growth rate of seven per cent per year. but the methods used were those of clearcutting the forests, exhausting its topsoil and selling off precious non-renewable mineral wealth.

In other words we are living in what some ecologists have dubbed a Potemkin village. When Catherine the Great of Russia went on tour, it is said that her chief minister Potemkin made sure that she passed through beautifully kept little villages, complete with hired yokels, so that she should know that he was governing her people well. But, alas, behind the hastily reared façades, there was squalor and poverty.

This deception is the more easily achieved since the arrival of Alfred Marshall's neoclassical economics. Adam Smith insisted on tangibility as the measure of wealth. Alfred Marshall maintained that the true measure was utility and that therefore the work of the City of London was as productive of wealth as a steelworks. Of course there is some truth in this but utility is much easier to juggle and deceive with, and if Potemkin could deceive with bogus villages, how much easier it was for Nick Leeson to juggle paper currency 'futures'.

Obviously some more accurate measure of what we actually receive in satisfaction, which also registers depletion of natural capital, is needed. There have been many attempts to produce such an index, and such attempts are a growth industry (with well over 200 institutions at work in the field) but as yet there is no widespread agreement as to which set of 'alternative indicators' is the best. One of the most interesting is the GPI or Genuine Progress Indicator produced by Redefining Progress, a San Francisco think tank; it shows that whereas American GDP has risen from $8,000 per head in 1950 to $17,000 per head in 1994, GPI rose from $5,600 in 1950 to peak at $7,600 in 1970 and then decline to $4,000 in 1994.[5]

Another such indicator is the Index of Sustainable Economic Welfare, pioneered by the Stockholm Environment Institute. Versions have been produced for the USA by Daly and Cobb and for the UK by Tim Jackson and Nic Marks.[6] This index takes into account the value of 'household labour', the deleterious effect of inequality in income and the cost of 'long-term environmental damage'. And yet another is the Human Development Index produced by UNICEF and UNDP.[7]

Producing indicators (like almost any worthwhile human activity) is both an art and a science. A key technique in producing a 'good' indicator is one that combines both accuracy and resonance. The first quality is self-evident. But almost as important is how much it means to the people whom it is intended to influence. The citizens of Seattle have chosen as one of their indicators one which means most to them because of their geography and history: 'the number of salmon runs in local rivers'. The inhabitants of the suburb in which I live might well choose as one of their resonant indicators the number of different birds seen in their gardens.

Another form of capital which becomes difficult to measure and which is much ignored, especially in societies where a great deal of value is placed on individualism, is social capital 'when people have been together for a long time developing shared norms, values and beliefs that enrich the way they live and work'.[8]

In almost all the arguments about indicators the answer to an either/or question is both/and. Accurate *and* resonant, bundled *and* unbundled: it is useful to 'bundle' indicators so that we get the overall picture but also important to look at each one separately — so that, in the words of Hazel

Henderson, 'ordinary citizens can clearly understand how they relate to goals in education, health, housing, political participation, cultural goals and environmental safety'.[9]

When we are estimating wealth we need to look not only at our income and expenditure accounts but also at the national and world balance sheets. In this field Ralf Dahrendorf et al have suggested an annual wealth audit whereby we keep our capital as well as our income under review.[10] Such a system has been applied to certain countries by the UN Statistical Division and has come up with some startling examples of depletion of capital where it was previously considered that economic growth was occurring.[11]

Any long term measure of satisfaction will rest on a capital basis of both natural and artificial resources. Hazel Henderson has produced a diagram rather like a layered cake showing how real wealth is made up.[12]

The bottom layer is the natural environment (which must be preserved at all costs); it consists of both sources and sinks. The next layer up is the co-operative social economy: unpaid housekeeping and parenting, mutual aid, the voluntary sector and production for use (e.g. allotments). Neither of these two layers employs anything but the minimum of actual cash.

Above this we get into the still social but now monetary economy: defence, health care (including sewerage), schools, infrastructure such as roads and railways, the administration of justice and government.

And only above this massive area of our life do we get to the 'private' area: employment, investment, savings and commercial consumption.

But a lot of that last layer is fragile. Among the more robust components of our wealth are agricultural land, mineral deposits, forestry, trained and informed brainpower and enough of whatever it is that we use in easily transportable and exchangeable form to enable us to harness those resources. The last factor (usually money) will ideally come from savings representing foregone consumption of real resources rather than from anticipation of hypothetical future ones.

I say 'ideally' representing foregone consumption because one of our many economic sins is to borrow from the future and not the past, in the expectation that we will be paid back out of future profits. This is of course common commercial practice and is only viable in that field because of the corrupt system known as 'limited liability' which enables individuals to escape the consequences of their mistakes. This corruption should certainly be curbed in any case, since borrowing from the future is a main cause of inflation, besides assuming that there is a future which is broadly predictable from a knowledge of past history. Such an assumption is not valid in a period of paradigm change and will undoubtedly have to be more or less eradicated in a sustainable economy.

One of our main problems is that one real but limited form of wealth is time. It is limited because we only have an uncertain amount of it and how are we to use it? One way we keep this problem at bay is by defining out of existence certain types of problems that have a longer time-cycle. Another method of avoiding it is the treasuring of technology which 'saves time'. But what do we do with the time that we have saved? Too often we use it on employing other technology with which to save yet more time.

Technology as wealth

Technology is a real part of wealth, being the tangible fruit of human brain-power in the same way that grain is the edible fruit of the soil, but it does not follow from this that we should adopt all new technologies regardless of their effects, thinking that thereby we will automatically be increasing our wealth, any more than we should put into practice all the behaviour that we are capable of imagining.

Technology can be and often is used to reduce employment and to tame organised labour. Andrew Ure, the great apologist for the industrial revolution, claimed 'that when capital enlists science in her service, the refractory hand of labour will always be taught docility'.[13] Wendell Berry has produced a list of criteria to guide in the acceptance or otherwise of technology. New tools should be cheaper, smaller and better than the ones they replace. They should use less energy (preferably renewable) be repairable, locally made, and not do harm to ecosystems including the human family.

In a recent defence of international competitiveness against a strong attack by the economist Paul Krugman,[14] Lester C. Thurow claims that 'foreign competition simultaneously forces a faster change of economic change at home and produces opportunities to learn new technologies and new management practices that can be used to improve domestic productivity. Put bluntly, those who don't compete abroad won't be productive at home'.[15]

But if improving domestic productivity merely means producing more goods (which may be wanted but are not needed) more cheaply with fewer workers, thus achieving more unemployment, more poverty and more crime, it is hard to see who is the gainer except a few fat cats. 'Oh,' say the economists, 'that is none of our business. It is the job of the politicians to distribute the wealth; we merely tell you how to gain it'.

But in fact there is little or no extra wealth to distribute, there is only money — and while we are all grateful in the first instance if we are the recipients of some extra money, money is no substitute for wealth, as some winners of the National Lottery could tell us.

A useful first step would be to agree on indicators, 'but they will not alone support the key social and environmental dimensions of sustainability. For indicators to be fully effective demands a radical shake-up in the way in which key decisions are made'. (At the moment there is a feeling that many of the reports produced by nations for the UNCSD as the raw data for such indicators go to New York and are not even analysed).[8]

Wealth: the aesthetic component

And true wealth must contain, to return to Auden's definition of civilisation since wealth (as opposed to riches) and civilisation are symbiotic, a strong aesthetic element. Too many, even among self-styled 'ecological' economists, in their efforts to demonstrate that monetary values are a tool for everything, forget this element. In *The Journal of the Institute of The International Society for Ecological Economics* (Vol 13 No 3) there is an article which sets off the economic gain of insect control using pesticides against the economic cost (insect control loss) of killing songbirds! Shelley, thou shouldst be living at this hour! The world hath need of thee!

The fact is that to gain true wealth for the planet we need to ration our mining of non-renewable resources, administer our agriculture and forestry on a strictly sustainable basis, maintain biodiversity, conserve non-renewable energy, make the most by education and training of the enormous capabilities of humankind and encourage an ethical climate which will persuade us to diminish the extremes between rich and poor both nationally and internationally.

1   Figure given at presentation given by the Director of Environment, Gloucestershire County Council (26/02/97)
2   Richard Douthwaite: *The Growth Illusion*.
3   David Korten: *When Corporations Rule the World*, p47.
4   Herman Daly in *Resurgence* 175.
5   *The Economist* 30/9/95 p63 (figures to the nearest round number).
6   *Measuring Sustainable Economic Welfare — A Pilot Index 1950-90* (New Economics Foundation); also an introductory leaflet on the same, *Growing Pains*.
7   Alex MacGillivray and Simon Zadek: *Accounting for Change*.
8   UNDP: *Human Development Report 1966*, p75.
9   *Country Futures Indicators* 93.
10   Ralf Dahrendorf et al: *Report on Wealth Creation*.
11   *Human Development Report 1996*, p63.
12   Hazel Henderson: *Paradigms in Progress* (Berrett-Koehler).
13   Quoted by Kirkpatrick Sale in *Rebels Against the Future*.
14   Paul Krugman in *Foreign Affairs* M/A 1994.
15   Lester C. Thurow in *Foreign Affairs* J/A 1994.

Chapter 5

Agriculture

Agricultural life is out of control. Being tied to the global market is like going out every morning and betting your farm on the horses.

Anon

'Gardening [as a subject in rural schools] is not very popular with the teachers because they find that the children know a great deal more about gardening than they do themselves, which has proved subversive to discipline.'

Adrian Bell in *Silver Ley*, c1930

THE JOURNEY ACROSS the bridge leading from conventional to ecological economics is one of considerable complexity involving as it does a change in the habits of human society at least as complete as that involved in the industrial revolution.

And while the industrial revolution has taken a considerable time to complete (and is not yet completed) — and was, at any one time, geographically limited — the ecological revolution must and will happen over a far shorter time span. It can do so because mass global communication means that when a major trend becomes accepted by the world's opinion formers there is no need for delay in implementing it everywhere and the pressures for the whole world to join the new trend will become very strong. This will be the more so if the new trend 'goes with the grain' and encourages, rather than uproots, local diversity and dispersed power.

It is becoming increasingly obvious that this revolution is bound to occur, as our knowledge of the problems we face increases. Such knowledge has increased every year in our own lifetimes, together with an awareness of the time needed to effect a turnaround (comparable in its way to the time involved in turning a vast oil-tanker around at sea.)

But if the complexity and time scale are bound to be formidable, nevertheless there are areas in which it must be possible as well as vital to establish bridgeheads by taking fairly swift action which will secure some degree of safety for the following troops.

And at the same time we must pay attention to a 'right direction' approach to more long term problems. Such an approach is based on the knowledge that while there are distant goals which we cannot achieve in the immediate future, nevertheless we must be careful that, as far as possible, we do not do things now which will make our task then more difficult.

The most important of the areas in which we can establish our bridgeheads is in the use of land. Land, water and air are the basic building bricks of our ecology and in this and the next chapter we will be looking at the use of land. We shall also discuss our use of the seas for fishing.

Land is a basic and as such there will always be competing demands on it which economics has got to sort out. We must examine the possible methods of doing this later in this chapter but on the way we would do well to cast a cursory glance over the main areas of demand: agriculture, forestry and bio-diversity.

Following our pattern of dealing with the most basic matters first even if they are not the most obvious, let us look now at biodiversity.

Biodiversity

> There is not much satisfaction in contemplating a world with scarcely a place where a wild shrub or flower could grow without being eradicated as a weed in the name of improved agriculture.
>
> John Stuart Mill

> It must be taken as a cardinal responsibility that we do not destroy what we cannot create and do not yet comprehend.
>
> R. J. Goodland and H. S. Irwin

Biodiversity is 'the wealth of life on earth, the millions of plants, animals and micro-organisms, the genes they contain and the intricate ecosystems they help build into the living environment. Biological diversity is simply the end result of four billion years of evolution.'[1]

Until recently humankind had hardly noticed the decline of biodiversity caused by the extinction of species. Of course we were aware of the relatively recent death of the dodo — indeed it has passed into our proverbial language — and of a few other highly noticeable mammals and birds, but it is not until fairly recently that we have noticed the widespread wastage that has been going on in what have seemed to us to be lesser species.

On a global level it is estimated that 2700 species are becoming extinct every year while in the UK 150 species have become extinct this century, of which about half were not known to exist elsewhere.

Now that we have noticed what is going on and are realising that it is important, we still tend to think in terms of a relatively small number of endangered species rather than of the immense gashes which may be being torn in the web of life. The authors of a modern *Paradise Lost*[2] compare us to a person jumping from the top of the Empire State Building who exclaims, 'So far, so good,' as he passes the twelfth floor. They also quote the analogy used by the Ehrlichs[3] of rivets in an aircraft wing. The removal of one rivet is unlikely to cause a crash, the removal of a great many is practically bound to ensure one, but it is virtually impossible to calculate the number of rivets which marks the fatal borderline point.

Nor is it possible, almost certainly, to achieve the ideal suggested by some that sustainable development demands that future generations inherit levels of biodiversity not less than those we inherited. Damage has gone too far unchecked and unrecognised and the task of even cataloguing our resources will take a very long time. Of course, one method might be to replace the extinct species with new genetically-engineered ones — but as far as I know, not even the most hubristic technological scientist has yet suggested this.

Nevertheless there are immediate steps which can be taken to try and limit the damage from the loss of species. One is to pinpoint and protect obviously endangered species and this, partly because of its appeal to the sentiment in humans, is already well under way.

The more long term measures, which nevertheless must be put on our 'right direction' list, include resistance to human cultural homogeneity, which tends also to homogenise natural habitats; and a campaign against world poverty, not least because 60% of the developing world's poorest people live in areas which can be classified as 'ecologically fragile'[4] and humans under pressure to survive will not spare many resources for what they see as non-essentials.

But enthusiastic networks of amateurs have proved important in saving genetic resources. In America the Seed Savers Exchange has conserved 1799 varieties of beans of which only 147 were to be found in the government collections. But government collections are important too and bureaucrats can be at least as dedicated. During the siege of Leningrad at least fourteen scientists died of starvation rather than raid the seedbanks in their care.[5]

There are plenty of good reasons for defending cultural diversity, not least that biological monocultures arise first and foremost from a 'monoculture of the mind'. The gene bank diminishes because locally useful plant varieties are eradicated or allowed to become extinct 'because the dominant knowledge systems discount the value of local knowledge and declare useful plants to be 'weeds'.[6]

This is a field in which we must be honest with ourselves and we must guard against being led off the straight and narrow road and down broad and slippery slopes of which 'substitution' is one and 'strict economic accounting' another. Of course we have to find substitutes for what we have lost and use substitutes as a means of conserving that which we are likely to lose, but we must realise that nothing is an adequate substitute for a single resource lost for ever and that substitution, although it is like appeasement in that it may buy time, is also likely to be, like appeasement, merely the first sacrifice of many to a voracious aggressor.

Equally of course we must use conventional economics to calculate where best to invest our resources of effort and wealth, but 'strict economic accounting' and 'cost effectiveness' are likely to produce scenarios which are aesthetically or morally unacceptable. Doubtless 'strict economic accounting' would have dictated that in the Second World War Britain should have sought peace terms after Dunkirk but we rejected that way of thinking then and we must reject it now in a far more vital war. The trouble with cost effectiveness is that it seldom finds a place for any values except monetary ones. In other words, it is a tool of classical not ecological economics.

Another insidious temptation is to adopt policies which appear to solve problems but which are in fact inherently unsound. One of these is the importation of species which seem as if they are adding to local biodiversity when in fact they are endangering it by upsetting the local ecological balance.

Yet another such temptation was an overemphasis of the importance of 'the Green Revolution' which, while promising much more food and delivering a large amount, eventually delivered disturbing alterations in ecological balance.[7] As a rule of thumb it is as well to bear in mind that there are no free lunches and that so-called miracle solutions probably aren't!

To reject the short cuts and aim for the right kind of progress involves considerable investment in knowledge. Every country must be helped to catalogue its biodiversity so that it can protect it. This is a major task but an urgent one. As the old staff college saying has it, 'Time spent in reconnaissance is seldom wasted'!

The use of land

> That land is a community is the basic concept of ecology, but that land is to be loved and respected is an extension of ethics. That Land yields a cultural harvest is a fact long known but latterly often forgotten.
>
> A. Leopold: *A Sand Country Almanac*

Alongside and contributing to biodiversity, the next most important task is to look at the use of land and indeed at the question of its ownership. I think that it is correct to state that the only culture in which land is held to be completely at the disposal of its owner is the present capitalist one (and then probably only in its Anglo-Saxon form). In every other culture the 'owner' is held to be merely a steward, whether for God, society or his family depending on the person's personal beliefs and the culture of their society. And a number of interesting schemes for taxation have been based on the right of the community to charge rent for the land, from Thomas Paine in *Agrarian Justice* (1797) to contemporary suggestions that a Citizen's Income should be funded out of a land tax.

The most obvious use of land is for the production of food. But there are competing demands which cannot be ignored. Among these are forestry and land for human settlements such as towns and cities.

Probably the most important step in the allocation of land in most people's priorities is to secure humanity's food supplies. We are fortunate in that our abuse of the planet is still in its early (although we hope also its late) stages and that there is no immediate threat of world famine, although the distribution of food supply is so skewed that large proportions of humanity are dangerously undernourished. The reasons for this are, like those for almost every other ill catalogued in this book, both complex and simple and find their expression in what Wendell Berry has called 'The Food System' which 'is firmly grounded on the following principles:

(1) Food is important mainly as an article of international trade.

(2) It does not matter what happens to farmers.

(3) It does not matter what happens to the land.

(4) Agriculture has got nothing to do with 'the environment'.

(5) There will always be plenty of food, for if farmers don't grow it from the soil then scientists will grow it in tanks.

(6) There is no connection between food and health. People are fed by the food industry which pays no attention to health, and are healed by the health industry which pays no attention to food.'[8]

But most opinion formers in educated elites in the developed world and almost all the inhabitants of the undeveloped world know that in the real world none of that is true and that therefore the 'Food System' has to be abolished in favour of something which is rooted in real facts and which is therefore a great deal more ecological.

Agriculture

The basic objective of farming in a Europe now alert to environmental, animal welfare and social problems remains to produce healthy food in suitable quantities [i.e. not for dumping on world markets] at a price that reflects its true cost.

Farming Can Have a Civilised Future
(A discussion paper produced by the Small Farmers Association)

In the planet's housekeeping two kinds of physical capital are involved, natural and artificial. When people become aware of fish as good to eat (natural capital) they also becomes aware of the need for fish hooks and nets (artificial capital) and their harvest of natural capital is to a considerable extent limited by the supply of the artificial capital. Later on when the fish hooks have evolved into trawlers fitted with deep refrigeration, the harvest may be limited by the diminishing of the natural capital by the application of the artificial. Natural and artificial capital are neither necessarily interchangeable, nor mutually supportive.

The ability of artificial capital to limit or diminish natural capital can be seen in a large number of areas, including forestry, but perhaps the most obvious is in the area of food. Feeding the world seems to have been nudged gently down from the number one place in international ecological concern, a move perhaps not unconnected with the fact that this particular threat is not at the moment real to the most powerful developed nations. So also, in considering the problems of feeding the world, the actual physical production of food has slid down the list of priorities in favour of problems such as distribution and purchasing power.

World hunger?

The world's supply of grain today could provide one and a half times the amount of calories the world needs. But in the time that the population of the world next doubles the supply of grain will not increase by anything like that amount. It might even decrease; at the very best it will increase arithmetically while the population increases algebraically. The optimists assume that this problem will be solved by biotechnology. But the director of research at one of the world's largest seed suppliers says, 'No breakthroughs are in sight. Biotechnology, while essential to progress, will not produce sharp upward swings in yield potential except for isolated crops in certain situations'.[9]

And there are reasons to think that any gains from that source may be offset by losses from soil degradation and loss of irreplaceable topsoil, diminishing irrigation and the heavy loss of cropland that occurs when countries that are already densely populated begin to industrialise,[10] not to mention the problems of nutrient recycling caused by moves to the cities. Cornell University researchers estimate that 10 million hectares of productive arable land are already being abandoned each year due to severe degradation.[11] In addition, the supply of soil nutrients diminishes as decreasing supplies of wood are replaced as fuel by cattle dung: the alternative, if we plant the 150 million hectares which Brown and Kane calculate to be necessary if firewood shortage is to be eradicated, hydrological stability restored and soil stabilised,[12] will be some serious loss of cropland.

It is true that there is a certain reservoir of available fertile cropland. Europe and America have both 'set aside' land in order to keep production down and there is a large acreage devoted to crops which are either not needed or are positively harmful — such as tobacco (or poppies for heroin). But this reservoir is not inexhaustible. In the US, the greatest grainbasket in the world, over a quarter of irrigated farmland is watered by depleting aquifer levels, a practice which will have to stop and, indeed, be reversed.

Because of the absence of serious famine at the present time the problem of the total supply of food is on the back burner for the time being. But the trouble with putting things on the back burner, as some of us amateur cooks know to our cost, is that you go out of the room to do urgent things and return to find that the water has boiled away and you have an inedible dinner and a ruined saucepan. Or to put it in classical ecological terms it invokes the parable of the weed on the pond which doubles daily, but which is not seen as a menace until halfway through the day on which it first covers half the pond, which is also the day before it covers the whole pond. The pond attendant then does some rapid calculations and panics.

That is not to say that distribution and purchasing power, which have taken the place of famine as 'problems', are not important. The main reason for 'famine' is poverty: people *cannot afford* to buy the food that exists. During the potato famine in Ireland in the last century, the relief boats bringing in food to the Irish ports for the hungry were outnumbered by the boats steaming out exporting food. The apparent paradox was caused by the fact that the first lot of ships were carrying food to be given away, while the second lot carried food which had to be paid for.

The world supply of grain (as mentioned above) could provide one and a half times the amount of calories the world needs. But 40% of it is at the present time fed to animals because the owners of livestock can afford to pay higher prices than the undernourished of the Third World. One result of this is that 22% of the world's population are responsible for the consumption of more than 60% of the world's grain supply.

But there are worrying signs that *actual shortage* of food may be on the agenda again. The forecasters in the FAO (Food and Agriculture Organisation) say that the graphs are cheerful but they are mainly economists who extrapolate forecasts in straight lines, while nature tends to work in sigmoid curves, and if you extrapolate

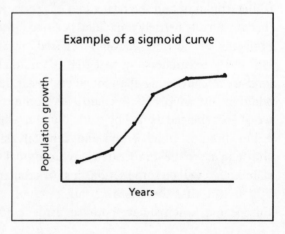

Example of a sigmoid curve

a straight line from the dynamic part of a sigmoid curve your results will be appallingly wrong.

The two main triggers for famine may be the fall in the level of aquifers, often caused by the presence of large cities such as Los Angeles and Beijing, and the ascent up the food chain of the diet of such countries as China. Henry of Navarre (Henri IV of France) wanted no peasants in his kingdom to be so poor that they could not have a chicken in their pot every Sunday. But a chicken in your pot every Sunday, especially if accompanied by a bottle or two of beer, puts an immense strain on grain supplies. Chickens are poor converters of grain and cattle are even worse.

Although there seems to be no present threat of the amount of food available not matching the basic demand, that is not likely to continue for long. Lester Brown and the Worldwatch Institute have pointed out the threat caused by China's growing demands as the eating habits of its enormous population move up the food scale. The size of this extra demand will depend on whether China follows the classic development pattern and builds more roads and more heavy industry, thus consuming large tracts of agricultural land, or whether it moves as quickly as possible into the electronic age and at the same time builds railways and cycle tracks rather than roads. But rise its food demands will and that will have a disruptive economic and political effect on the world. One has only to look at the traumas caused by rising oil prices in the seventies. 'There are, after all, substitutes for oil. But there are no substitutes for food... At the international level, climbing food prices could lead to potentially unmanageable inflation, abrupt shifts in currency exchange rates, widespread political instability ... and a spreading flow of hungry migrants across national borders.'[13]

But the first problem of world hunger and malnutrition still stems from the unequal distribution of wealth. And much more food would be available for direct consumption if countries did not feel that they had to grow cash crops to earn hard currency in order to buy imports or pay off debt.

Much of the best land in Ethiopia is devoted to growing coffee, in a world awash with coffee, in order to earn foreign currency. Sub-Saharan countries paid $12 billion in debt servicing in 1993. According to UNICEF the same amount would provide health and education services, safe water and other basic needs to every person on the continent; alternatively, if applied to land redistribution, it would provide the land with which peasants could farm and feed themselves and their neighbouring towns along the pattern of Europe before the industrial revolution.

Feeding ourselves

An agricultural policy for Britain

Britain's agriculture is increasingly polarised. 'At one extreme are some 6000 big farms that generate a quarter of all farm profits. At the other are about 100,000 smallholdings of less than 50 acres each that are run as little more than hobbies by people with other sorts of income. In the middle are another 100,000 farms from 25 to 250 acres that are struggling to survive as viable concerns. For many the future is bleak. Their best hope may lie in partnership with land management companies or larger neighbours'.[14]

The first group are to be treated, if not with hostility at least with the gravest suspicion. They regard farming as an industry, not as a profession or as a stewardship and although they can be bribed to be environmental in their behaviour they will never be environmental in their outlook. For them the bottom line is always expressed in pounds and pence.

The second group are to be cherished. It is true that at one extreme many of them merely like a paddock where they can keep the children's ponies, but at the other they represent the way of life which one British agricultural minister attacked when he asked his German counterpart why European agriculture should rotate round the farms worked in the summer evenings and weekends by the Munich car workers and their families — and received the devastating answer that if we had the same system there would be fewer strikes at Cowley. Those, of course, were the days when we had a car industry in which to have strikes. And this system can also be seen to work well in Japan.

The third group is the one which really needs a farming system that pays, and we will turn our attention to what is needed to achieve that in a moment.

The fourth group, the professional land managers, are the first group writ large with knobs on. For while many of the first group were people or the sons and daughters of people who had a real attachment to the land, most traces of this have died out in those whose aim, sometimes even achieved, is solely to earn a return of 25% per annum on capital.

How then do we make certain that we can have a thriving farming and rural economy? The solution is simple although the task of achieving it is immensely difficult, and the first step is to understand that Britain is not nearly as rich a country as we are used to thinking it. Our seeming riches come from many different factors some of which stem from frittering away true wealth in favour of GNP as conventionally defined. Just as the whole industrial world has gone on chalking up economic growth at the same time as true welfare is declining, so we, an over-populated country, have gone on neglecting our rural sector in the firm assurance that somehow free trade will feed us cheaply. Well, it won't! At least not in a world working with a sustainable economy and not if countries are therefore not permitted to have 'footprints' which spread beyond their own borders or those of the close colleagues with whom they share an economy.

The real need is to get every nation or bloc of nations to feed itself. In Britain, especially England, that is difficult if not impossible because of our over-population. But that is a very good reason why the existing machinery of the Common Agricultural Policy could be useful. At the time of writing the CAP is a shambles and there is absolutely no reason to think that it will not still be a shambles in ten years time. 'There are still large market imbalances in many of the CAP product sectors like cereals, dairy products and meat. Consumers still face unreasonably high prices, adding over £10 to the weekly shopping bill of a family of four and affecting low income consumers particularly badly. The CAP still swallows up at least half the EU budget even though less than 6% of the workforce is employed in agriculture. And much taxpayers' money is wasted on the export, storage or destruction services.'[15]

But if we make a success of the formation of trading blocs such as the EU and use them as our bases, on the assumption that the bonds are sufficiently reliable that we are prepared to risk our national security on them, Britain would be let off the hook of self-sufficiency, even though it would probably be in the interests of our long term health as a country to strive for it. But the idea that the CAP should be extended eastwards, thus taking in the fertile agricultural lands of central Europe following the break-up of the Soviet bloc, would be a real case of biting off considerably more than could be chewed.

One very good, though currently neglected, reason for being able to feed ourselves is the basic one of national security. Those of us who are my age have lived through a period when it was necessary to try to feed ourselves (and more or less to succeed) and although it is less likely that we shall have to do so again because of the political union of Western Europe and because of the nature of modern war, no one can count on it.

If the future which this book is forecasting fails to emerge, the alternative will involve some hefty mass migrations from Africa, Eastern Europe and Asia into the EU, which even the English Channel may not stop.

We seem to have become so arrogant about our trading ability that we have forgotten the lessons of self-sufficiency which some other countries still understand, even in a world of GATT. Fritz Schumacher in a splendid passage in *Good Work* pictures King Faisal describing to Sheikh Yamani how the best way to store the riches of oil is to leave it in the ground, since then the only way you can lose it is by being invaded and then at least you can fight. If you sell it and invest in another country's industry you can always have your holdings expropriated. What you have physically got you can usually keep. What is in the physical hands of others is not nearly so safe.

A national food policy

Nor is it to be condemned as an absurdity of the 'nanny state' if countries develop their own food policies, any more than if they operate a health service. After all the two interact. The Norwegian food policy adopted in the mid-seventies aims to:

(1) encourage a health-promoting diet;

(2) promote domestic food production and reduce food imports;

(3) promote agricultural development in the country's less advantaged regions while preserving the environment;

(4) contribute to world food security, promoting world food production and consumption in poor countries.

It seems to me that such a programme could and should be adopted wholesale by all countries including our own.[16]

It will have to be borne in mind that the fourth aim of the Norwegian food policy involves tailoring diet to an agricultural footprint. The more meat that we eat the more grain we consume indirectly. In 1994, producing the 30 million tons of pork consumed in China required 120 million tons of grain. The world's total grain exports in that year, when Chinese diet was only just beginning to move up the food chain, were slightly over 200 million tons.[17]

In sustainable terms the British cannot afford to consume much meat.

---

1   Worldwide Fund for Nature: *The Importance of Biological Diversity*, 1995.
2   Edward Barbier, Joanne C. Burgess and Carol Folke (Earthscan 1994).
3   P. R. and A. H. Ehrlich: *Extinction: The Causes and Consequences of the Disappearance of Species* (Random House 81).
4   H. J. Leonard: *Environment and the Poor: Development Strategies for a Common Agenda* (Transaction Books, New Brunswick 89).
5   C. Fowler and P. Mooney: *The Threatened Gene*.
6   Vandana Shiva: *Monocultures of the Mind*.
7   G. R. Conway and E. B. Barbier: *After the Green Revolution* (Earthscan 1990).
8   Wendell Berry in *Resurgence*, 165.
9   Donald Duvick quoted by Brown and Kane in *Full House*.
10 Brown and Kane, p27.
11 Brown and Kane. There can be an added problem if certain cultures do not yet understand what is the necessary action. It is said that the Chinese have no word for 'topsoil' and subsequently their bureaucrats do not realise the importance of moving and reusing it when they build, though it is a fair bet that their farmers do.
12 Brown and Kane.
13 Lester Brown: *Who Will Feed China?*, p123.
14 *The Times* countryside correspondent.
15 National Consumer Council: *Agricultural policy in the European Union*, 9/95.
16 Geoff Tansey and Tony Worsley in *The Food System*.
17 *World Policy Journal*, Spring 96.

Chapter 6

Forestry and land use

A culture is no better than its woods.

W. H. Auden

THE SECOND CLAIMANT for land use is forestry. We tend unconsciously to give to forestry less attention than we do to agriculture and to fisheries. Even the most urban of us knows that food comes eventually from the farm or the sea. But the purpose of trees is not so immediately apparent. We like to see trees of course, especially 'those pink ones in the Spring'. Some of us are not entirely sure that we 'shall never see a poem lovely as a tree'[1] but we are prepared to concede that it is an arguable point.

Looking round the office in which I am working, I am far from sure which bits of furniture are wood and which are plastic; as a city dweller I am no longer allowed to use wood as fuel even if I wanted to, except in very specialised stoves, and it takes more of an effort to associate my daily paper with a tree than it does to associate the milk that I put on my cornflakes with a cow.

This is one of the most dangerous alienations of Western people from nature, since it means that the cause of forests, while understood intellectually, lacks for most of us the emotional kick to move it up our agendas.

But forestry is important. It is immediately so for those who live in the Third World and it is essential for the ecology of the world as a whole.

For many in the Third World it provides the firewood with which they cook, warm themselves (and sometimes even use defensively as Mowgli did to repel Shere Khan).[2] It also provides building materials and furniture, more basically and obviously than in the West.

For all of us forests are fundamentally important and we should make sure that we are able to 'see the wood for the trees' and respond on the large as well as on the small scale. Forests are the home of perhaps half the biodiversity of the world. They are the globe's buffer against greenhouse warming, they are a principal moderator of local climate extremes, they filter the air, prevent floods and droughts, protect fisheries, and they secure the soil.[3]

And so it is for very good reasons that we should be appalled by the immense decline in the forest cover of the world which has occurred since the industrial revolution and which has accelerated enormously in our lifetime.

When we start thinking what we should do about it, as in the British Government's recent plan to double the woodland in Britain, we realise that in an over-populated planet and an over-populated country *forestry and agriculture compete for land*. It is true that nature has thoughtfully provided a lot of land which is suitable for forestry but which would make bad agricultural land, but there still remains a real problem. And such woodland as is being restored is often lacking in quality and richness, being biologically impoverished stands of commercial timber or the kind of suburban woodland, rampant all over the United States and in the home counties of Britain, which has been planted mainly for the not very ecological purpose of shielding the rich from the eyes of their neighbours (and indeed of protecting their own eyes from the view of others less aesthetically housed).

We cannot avoid the fact that proper woodlands which are going to serve the purposes we have listed above, while they can certainly be cropbearing through coppicing etc, cost more than they are worth when valued in classical economic terms. It is only in terms of ecological economics, with its global view and long time scale, that they are worthwhile. And in the race to keep feeding the world and to keep it healthy until population growth is first halted and then reversed, some very difficult choices are going to have to be made.

On a global scale, there is a clear first duty to try and save what remains of the rainforests and this may, as long as we are running on the present economic system, involve the richer countries of the world paying some of the poorer countries to ensure that this happens (yet another demand on countries which are going to have to face a much less 'rich' future). But a possible way of making this less painful while still effective may be in the form of debt remission — less painful because much of the debt may have been written off already for all practical purposes, yet effective because there is evidence that reducing debt actually can reduce deforestation.[4]

An added spur to saving some of the forests is that it will involve the preservation of some indigenous peoples in a way of life which many of them want to preserve. The best guardians of the forests might well be those who have lived with them and who can be helped, but not dictated to, from outside. While I realise that there are major differences between the tropical forests and the cedars of Lebanon it is interesting to note that the deforestation of Palestine followed hard, some scientists think, on the deportation of the Children of Israel into the Babylonian captivity.

Land reform

> Let us set a limit to the extent of land an individual may own, give the
> excess land to those who really need it and put a stop to the concentra-
> tion of land ownership in the hands of the few.
>
> Tung Chung Shu, 140 BC

One of the many evils of the unregulated capitalist system is the reinforce-
ment of the idea that land can be *owned*. Most thinking landlords and farmers
have known differently. Alongside an often fiercely proprietorial attitude to
land has gone the last remnant of the idea that the land eventually belongs to
God, or at the very least to the community, and that the landlord or farmer is
merely a steward. The breakdown of belief in both God and community has
led in some people to only the fiercely proprietorial attitude remaining, and
in a sustainable economy such an attitude can no longer be tolerated. The
landowner cannot exercise absolute rights over land since it has to be treated
in such a way that the welfare of succeeding generations (and not merely of
that person's descendants) will be ensured.

With the demands on land surface made by agriculture, forestry and
increasing population, it is clear that every society needs at least a machinery
for land-use allocation and probably a policy for how to use it as well. The
alternative is to leave the matter to the 'market' — not a good idea for a great
many reasons, one of the chief of which is the power exerted in the market
by those who have possession (it being nine points of the law) at the
moment, as opposed to the general body of the citizenry, and the propensity
of the former to employ it for short term profit.

To adapt slightly Fritz Schumacher's three principles of human work: the
three tasks of agriculture are 'to keep man in touch with living nature, of
which he is and remains a highly vulnerable part; to humanise and ennoble
man's wider habitat; and to bring forth the foodstuffs and other materials
which are needed for a becoming life'.[5] And if that is true (and I believe it to
be so) it will quickly be seen that if agriculture is to play a part in our civilisation (and it must), the larger the proportion of people in touch with the land
the better. As we begin to think holistically we will not be surprised to find that
the task of providing the world with food demands the same thing.

China has increased its agricultural output dramatically by improving
farmers' incentives and placing land under the management of households
rather than communes, although the reforms occurred so quickly that much
useful machinery was jettisoned in the process.[6] What is needed is practical
(not ideological) co-operatives and intermediate technology. And although
China had the enormous, if morally complex, advantage of doing away with
landlordism in an earlier revolution in order to introduce Maoist collectivism,

it is extremely likely that peasant farming will eventually become the pattern for maximum food production all over the world. It has always been common sense that smallholdings produce the most food per hectare;[7] the reason that they have become unpopular in the West over a relatively short period of time is that they have produced it at a high cost of expensive labour and that they are not suited to making the rich richer. But now that the world has begun to realise that it is natural capital which is the limiting factor in a finite world, all this must change.

Major land reform is by no means as rare as those who live in countries where it has never occurred might think. It has of course occurred in almost all countries where there has been real revolution, as in France, Russia and China, as well as in those where revolution has been feared, as in Ireland in 1903 under the benevolent tutelage of George Wyndham.

It was also widely introduced in South East Asia, for instance in Japan and Taiwan, and attempted in South Korea and South Vietnam, usually under American influence, unlikely though that may sound today.[8] The objectives have been mixed, sometimes involving the removal of a largely parasitical and sometimes absentee landlord class, sometimes as a way of spreading wealth, and often as a means of increasing the productivity of the land.

Ronald Herring in his study *The Political Economy of Agrarian Reform in South Asia*[9] (which might more accurately have been titled 'The Political Economy of Plans for Agrarian Reform in the Indian Sub-Continent') quotes the World Bank as saying that the net economic effects of land reform are unknowable. But it goes on to say that 'the strongest economic case for land reform is in terms of development; if development means anything at all, it means the alleviation of poverty, unemployment, hunger and backwardness'. That's not a bad recommendation from a far from avant-garde institution, while Ambassador Chester Bowles suggested[10] that both the defeat of Chiang Kai Shek on the Chinese mainland and the outbreak of civil war in South Vietnam might have been avoided by land reform: some substance is given to the former suggestion by the sudden conversion of the Kuo Min Tang to the idea when forced back on to Formosa.

Occasionally, as in Mexico, the results have been bad, but in that case rights to the land were not accompanied by access to credit, tools and seeds. It was an incomplete programme. In Cuba the results were mixed. But on the whole the record is encouraging, sometimes as in Japan and South Korea being credited with stimulating and. far-reaching effects on the whole economy (the South East Asian miracle).

Small farms

The size of a holding which is necessary for secure subsistence depends on a large number of factors. In her fascinating book about Ladakh in Kashmir

Helena Norberg-Hodge states that at the time she first started visiting the region in 1976 the average family holding was well under 4 hectares and a comfortable living was achieved on this.[11]

In Britain, a move to smaller farms could easily be achieved by fiscal means. There would be immense gains in terms of the repopulation of the countryside and in redistributing wealth, since at the moment subsidies tend to be given to the rich. Eighty eight per cent of the £2.2 billion which supported British Agriculture in 1994 went to the richest 20% of farmers.

Of course there would be costs both economic and other. The economic ones would start to be paid by the redirection of the money which is poured into the wrong kind of agriculture today. Other costs might well be most obvious in a continuing suburbanisation of the countryside, with a real ecological threat to wildlife, particularly the larger and more obvious forms. The RSPB has commissioned an interesting study of this question.[12]

Small farms should of themselves be environmentally beneficial if only through the fact that each square metre is precious and that therefore the competing claims of productivity and, say, species diversity can be weighed up. And of course they are more productive on any criterion except that of labour. G.A. Squires in his chapter 'The Small Farmer on the Land' in *The Small Farmer* recounts cropping 6cwt of strawberries from 'maiden plants' in 1944 and goes on to say that one or two people had suggested that if he had 'an acre or two like that' he could make a fortune, to which the answer was that if he had an acre he could not possibly 'do' them so well and that anyway he had no intention of becoming a strawberry specialist. 'Variety is the spice of smallholding life'.[13]

And small farms encourage the humane use of animals; the abandonment of factory farming, the reversal of the process which was 'to change the dairy cow from the family companion animal she became after domestication and through all of man's subsequent history into the appropriate manufacturing unit of the twentieth century for the efficient transformation of unprocessed feed into food for man'.

Indeed Professor Boutflour, one of the apostles of modern farming when I was taking my agricultural degree at the beginning of the fifties, went on record as saying that 'no form of big farming, mechanised or otherwise can compete against peasantry. Even in countries of large areas, like Argentine, the man who has been able to see bad times through is the smaller man'.

The worldwide pattern of landowning is extremely varied although everywhere that the large corporations have got a foothold, rural population and small farms are under threat.

But even in the great monoculture prairies of America there are signs that a desire to care for the land is fighting back. One of the troubles is that the great aquifers are being depleted by monoculture, they take generations to replenish and the solution of some is just to give up and return to 'grass, Indians and buffalo, as God perhaps intended'. But others are more inspired and both cattle and telecommuting whizz-kids from California have been sighted on the High Plains.

But though there may be pros and cons in the ecological balance nothing could be worse than the wildlife massacre caused by the present system over the last fifty years. For this reason among many others, it is important that land reform be accompanied by a population policy which takes off some of the pressure.

There would be other gains too. The suicide of farmers is twice the national average according to Jules N. Pretty,[14] one of the reasons for which must be loneliness. 'There are vast tracts of land' in Suffolk, where journalist and small farmer Paul Heiney lives, 'where no man sets foot year in year out,' although the occasional representative of the species (and it should be emphasised that there are very few other species in large numbers either) appears on a mammoth tractor.

It cannot be denied that here, as in other fields, ecology may be the enemy of environmentalism. For many people will resent the restrictions on access to farms which will have to be stricter even than those proposed by the land-lords today, since greater production per acre calls for greater protection.

As it is, the chairman of the Ramblers Association can say, 'The time has now passed when the path-blocking, anti-access, criminal land-owning community can get away with excluding the public from huge tracts of the countryside'. And it may not be much consolation (though it should be) that the restrictions will be correctly justified as in the common good. Of course the friction may and should be reduced by an increased understanding of the importance of what farmers are doing, as a result of a lively localised agri-cultural economy.

Implementing these reforms will not be easy and it may be that Britain will be one of the last countries to achieve it, partly because of our largely unpar-alleled system of landlordism. And the road will be strewn with the wreckage caused by the GATT agricultural agreements. However, one good thing came out of the Uruguay agreement: a 'ministerial decision' protecting food aid (in itself of dubious value) included an undertaking 'to give full consideration in the context of their aid programmes to requests for the provision of technical and financial assistance to least-developed and net food-importing developing countries.[15]

Luckily, we are likely to find allies (or rather pacemakers) in the other coun-tries of Europe. It is virtually impossible to name a member of the European Union (or indeed of the candidate states) which does not have a strong, respected and still politically influential tradition of peasant-farming.

A short but useful step on the way might be a ceiling on agricultural subsidies based on acreage as opposed to labour employed, thus putting a pressure on landowners to reduce the size of their holdings and encouraging in a practical way more labour on the land.

Some 5055 English farmers received over £50,000 each in subsidies in 1994. To pay those who were eligible only up to that sum would save £201m. A ceiling of £30,000 would save £350m. The Small Farmers Association document quoted above suggests three immediate changes: (1) a ceiling on the total subsidy any one farmer can receive; (2) tapering rates of subsidies; (3) simpler and more universal environmental payments.

Another help would be a Land Bank dedicated to providing farmers with limited amounts of capital at low interest rates. In 1990 farm debt reached £7 billion and 6000 British farmers stopped farming.[16] Many had been caught in a trap of debt not unlike that of the thirties. Modern intensive farming has always demanded that you have advanced large scale machinery. When you have bought that, you then have to buy the acres to provide enough work for advanced large scale machinery to do. You are then heavily in hock to the bank and when the price of land goes down your debts are not even covered.

The counsel of perfection is that you do not get into debt in the first place. A sustainable economy would not allow you to borrow against future prospects, only on the security of past saving. But, short of that situation of the future, the next best thing is that farmers stick to *extensive* (non-intensive) farming on a manageable holding, use appropriate technology and have access to low-interest capital for these purposes (and these only). An added bonus would be serious grants for conversion to organic farming and for staying in it.[17]

In the first instance a reform of the Common Agricultural Policy may have to move obliquely towards a situation where it aims to maximise production through non-intensive farming (not a contradiction in terms) and through protection of the environment before it makes the final rebellion and establishes protection for home produced foodstuffs alongside measures to restrain agricultural exports.

'Agriculture's most important contribution to rural development is no longer the production of feed and food, but the protection and promotion of rural amenity, ecological integrity and cultural identity', said H. von Meyer in a paper prepared for an East-West interparliamentary meeting in May 1992 — and while that will no longer be strictly true in a more hungry world it is a good start and the direction in which the EU (including Britain) must move. The SAFE alliance has come up with 10 objectives for a sound policy for agriculture, which include:

- being supportive of rural communities and halting the decline of employment;
- not jeopardising the health of producers or consumers;
- not reducing soil fertility and being sustainable;
- conserving the countryside and its wildlife; and
- the welfare of farm animals.

At the same time von Weizsacker suggests that a strict enforcement of environmental controls and a transparency to the consumer about processes, including genetic engineering, would be a good start.[18]

Organic farming

Peasant farming tends towards organic farming and there is increasing evidence that we need more organic food. Professor Crawford, winner of the Swiss International Award for Modern Nutrition, says that British mothers producing low birthweight babies, which carry a greater risk of disability and reduced brain function, are malnourished not only because they are eating the wrong kind of food but because of the way it is produced. Intensive agriculture has diluted the nutritional value of food.

Organic farming is also a safeguard against some threatened human nutritional ills. At the time of writing it may be that the scares about some diseases carried by meat are not entirely justified, but as the Prince of Wales has put it, there are many farmers who feel that it simply is 'not right to be feeding herbivores with the rendered remains of other herbivores'.[19]

There is on the face of it every incentive for a farmer with a very small holding, not enjoying a high cash flow, to keep at least a few livestock to produce manure which can be ploughed back into the soil and to avoid the use of chemicals — with all their various hazards which we will examine briefly in the next chapter.

And the preservation of a good soil structure for fertility is best ensured by the use of sewage from cities to feed the soil immediately around it (as in China) from which the city should draw at least its fruit and vegetables — if not its fish supply, as in the sewage/algae/fishponds surrounding Calcutta.

Fisheries

In addition to farming, one of the great sources of food is fishing. If we are to feed the world while we are sorting out the population problem, we have got to act fast and drastically and put many of our practices into reverse. All the world's major fishing grounds are at or beyond their sustainable limits, according to the FAO.[20] The main reasons for this are that we have destroyed the coastal fishing of many countries and we have failed to regulate the deep-sea fishing of the oceans.

It is probably right that deep-sea fishing should be more or less industrialised although it must be properly policed and so supervised that overfishing and the wastage of fish (e.g. the catching of unwanted species by accident) are guarded against.

However a large proportion of the world's fishing has always been coastal and it and the communities which practised it should be revived where they have not already been irretrievably wrecked. Sometimes this proves possible: a recent Act of the British parliament, The Sea Fisheries (Shellfish) (Amendment) Act 1997, establishes an inshore lobster ranching industry complete with controls on over-fishing. This might well prove a model for other countries.[21]

There is a saying that 'if you give a man a fish you feed him for a day but if you teach him to fish you feed him for a lifetime'. To that might be added: 'And if you teach him to make his own fishing tackle you make him self-sufficient for ever and ensure him worthwhile employment'.

And if it be asked whether the 'artificial' employment of people in fishing is justified when feeding the world with fish could be done more 'efficiently' by putting them out of work, the answer is that only by employing whole communities in fishing can you assure that conservation of stocks which is necessary to feed the world.

Conservation of water

A vital early beachhead in achieving agricultural and resource sustainability is the conservation of water. Those of us who live in Britain are lucky to live on an island which is well supplied with water — too well supplied, some of us think — but while water use in the UK is more or less on a sustainable basis, there are no grounds to think that this state of affairs is completely stable. There is every reason to incorporate water into the economic organisation of resources, thus reducing costs now and ensuring future control. That such measures as metering water are politically difficult because of their impact on poor families is, of course, yet another reason for dealing with the UK poverty situation.

But the world situation admits of no complacency. 1400 litres of water are needed to produce 1kg of corn, 40% of the world's population face chronic water shortages, and it is dirty water which in some countries causes 80% of illnesses.[22] The whole problem of food and water conservation is bound up together. Water scarcity depresses grain yields especially in the presence of hot summers.

1   Joyce Kilmer: *Trees*.
2   'Mowgli's Brothers' from Rudyard Kipling: *The Jungle Book* (1894).

3   Alan Thein Durning: Worldwatch Paper 117, *Saving the Forests: What will it take?*
4   J. R. Kahn and Judith A. McDonald: 'Third-world debt and tropical deforestation', in *Ecological Economics* 12: 1995 pp 107-23.
5   E. F. Schumacher: *Small is Beautiful*, p93.
6   William Hinton: *The Great Reversal* (Monthly Review Press) NY 1990.
7   For the proof see *Land Reforms in SE Asia* by Zahir Ahmed, p77, for the figures for Taiwan.
8   'Land Reform', in *Encyclopaedia Britannica*.
9   *Land to the Tiller,* Robert J Herring.
10   Foreword to *Land Reforms in South East Asia*, by Zahir Ahmed.
11   Helena Norberg-Hodge: *Ancient Futures: Learning from Ladakh* (Rider 1991).
12   *Small Farming and the Environment* by Clive Potter and Matt Lobley (RSPB 1992).
13   In H. J. Massingham: *The Small Farmer*, pp 114-5.
14   Jules N. Pretty: *Sustainability in a Rural Culture* (IEED).
15   Final act embodying the results of the Uruguay Round of Multi-lateral Trade Negotiations, Cm2570 05/94.
16   HRH The Prince of Wales: speech to Royal Agricultural Society of England 14/3/91.
17   There are grants for the first of these already in Britain but they could be part of a large scale policy and not just an optional extra subject to cuts the first time the Government needs to make savings.
18   *Agriculture and Environment in Europe*, quoted in *European Agriculture* by Ockenden and Franklin (A Chatham House Paper, 1995).
19   *The Times* 7/10/95.
20   World Watch Paper 126.
21   For the debate on this see House of Lords Hansard 577/35.
22   *UN Environmental Notes for Parliamentarians* (10/95).

Chapter 7

The steady state economy

IN PLANNING HOW we are to cross the bridge which leads from the classical economic system in which we find ourselves trapped to the system of ecological economics in which we must work if we and the planet are to survive, we must always keep firmly in our mind the nature of the place at which we hope eventually to arrive, even if at the beginning it is merely a distant green and gold blur on the horizon. The most important point is that we are not aiming to establish another dynamic economic system but rather a stable one: we are aiming in other words for *a steady state economy*.

That does not mean, as some will immediately think, that we want to move to some bland world where there will be no challenges. In this planet on which we find ourselves there will be more than enough challenge involved in maintaining a steady state, coming to terms with human nature and adapting to that evolution which is endemic to life. In the words of John Stuart Mill, who regarded the 'stationary state' of economics as a consummation devoutly to be hoped for, 'a stationary condition of capital and population implies no stationary state of human improvement. There would be as much scope for ever for all kinds of mental culture, and moral and social progress, as much room for improving the Art of Living and much more likelihood of it being improved, when minds cease to be engrossed by the arts of getting on'.[1]

Quality of life must become the aim of life rather than the amassing of a quantity of money. Wealth, health and the pursuit of happiness will become the targets; such goods as depend for their value on being scarce and therefore giving us a buzz because others cannot have them are not part of wealth and will therefore cease to be acceptable objectives.[2]

If that sounds easier said than done, it is. Money will never cease to be the objective for some. But we will become as adept as mediaeval schoolmen were at recognising and condemning greed in all its guises (first in ourselves!). Education has done wonders in getting us to accept greed as the mainspring of life but it can be employed in the other direction. Children are natural believers in ideals as we see today in their avid espousal of Green aims when they are exposed to them.

The abolition of poverty

One important ideal on which we must focus is the abolition of poverty. We have seen in our examination of wealth and riches that if we are to abolish poverty we must abolish riches because neither can exist without the other. In the place of both we are to put wealth. And one of the first steps in doing this is to spread money more evenly.

We have long known that the words of Francis Bacon, 'Money is like muck; of no use save it be thickly spread', are true, although a generation in the West which has never seen a muckheap or a well-manured field (and if they saw either would summons the farmer for creating a nuisance) may find it difficult to comprehend fully the force of the analogy.

Extremes of riches and poverty are inefficient; they place money in the hands of those who desire chiefly to buy luxuries while making it impossible for the needy to buy necessities. And our state of wealth for all must be built upon a foundation of necessities for all.

We must have taxation of resources rather than of earnings. This raises problems since it is difficult to make such taxation progressive (that is to say, to use it to reduce inequality) and therefore it is important to combine it with other measures which are progressive. Sometimes (but rarely) the two can be combined. It may, for instance become necessary in the cause of averting world hunger to tax ascents up the food-chain, that is to say to tax the consumption of meat and even to encourage vegetarianism. This will tax resources at the same time as taxing the rich rather than the poor shopper.

The distribution of power

And there will always exist the temptation to choose the short term benefit to ourselves over long term benefit to the community. For example we may allow out-of-town malls so that those of us who have cars can do our weekly shopping in a couple of hours rather than preserve town centres as true focuses of community and savers of energy.

In forging our programme we obviously have to think about the distribution of power, both as an objective and as a means — and as Ruskin pointed out to us in *Unto This Last*, power and riches are virtually synonymous since in the last resort riches are the means of commanding the labour of others.

Those who wield political power must be elected by, accountable to, and replaceable by the people over whom power is exercised. There should be sufficient central funding of political participation to ensure that the wealthy do not have a decisive advantage and to prevent the TNCs from purchasing votes as they do in America. (It should be born in mind that the GDPs of Austria and General Motors, South Africa and Royal Dutch Shell, and Yugoslavia and Toyota are roughly equal).

Ideally, everybody should possess sufficient autonomous economic power to guarantee their decent subsistence. Nobody should possess so much economic power as to make possible the coercion of others.

If redistribution of wealth is essential for the new economics, land reform is, as we have seen, at the very least desirable. Indeed universal small-scale ownership of all forms of capital is to be aimed at. It is ideally to be held in a mix of personal and co-operative or communal forms.

And together with redistribution of wealth must go devolution of power. Indeed the two automatically go together. Communist W. Bengal has recently very successfully devolved both power and money to village councils.

Guarding sources of energy

After the consideration of power, and overlapping with it, comes the conservation and control of energy which is the primary tool of all life. Energy cannot be recycled; once used it is dissipated. But its sources can be conserved and energy can be renewed from them.

And it is vitally important that energy is productively used and not wasted. The National Academies Policy Advisory group has concluded that in Britain 'a reduction in energy demand of more than 20% over the next twenty years would be achievable if only the readily available, existing technologies and best practices were universally applied. The changes concerned would take time, but would reduce costs to the householder, commerce and industry'.

We must make every effort to rely more on renewable energy. This may cost more both in cash and in our possible aesthetic dislike of (say) wind-farms, a reminder that ecology and environmentalism are not by any means the same thing. There are bills to pay for our previous bad behaviour.

One thing that we will not be able to afford is the immense guzzling of cheap oil by aeroplanes flying perishable commodities such as cut roses and food over vast distances. There has been recently a trade skirmish (it would be absurd to call it a trade war) between Italy and Canada over pasta. In the short term it had understandable features because of the special qualities of the grain produced in Canada. It was not quite as absurd as Danish pastries crossing each other in the air between Copenhagen and New York, when all that would be needed if it were not for the financial factor involved would be a fax exchange of recipes. Long term solutions for the pasta incident however should not be too difficult to find.

And in a world where energy is valued it would not be impossible (as it has been recently) to buy any asparagus except Spanish in supermarkets on the edge of that once great British market garden, the Vale of Evesham.[3]

It is of course quite clear that in this area as in others a lot of blame must be laid on our failure to control advertising. The achievement of the steady state economy is going to involve an education away from greed, and one of the most eminent figures in advertising has himself said, 'The essence of good advertising is not to inspire hope but to create greed'.[4]

Clearly we must find an equilibrium whereby we use as little as possible non-renewable energy as we struggle to reach a state of affairs where we need only use the (in the short term more expensive) renewable energy. Nuclear energy has seemed to many to be the way to fill the gap but it is an inherently centralised and dangerous energy source and far more expensive than its proponents would have had us believe.

The facts that it is centralised and therefore vulnerable and dangerous has led British Nuclear Fuels in the past to think it necessary to pry into the private lives of its employees right down to the level of the seamen on the ships removing waste,[5] and while there can legitimately be two opinions about the right to privacy in a sustainable society, their actions are a useful indicator of the level of the physical risks involved.

1   John Stuart Mill, quoted on p28 of Hermann Daly's Introduction to *Essays Toward a Steady-State Economy.*
2   For a full discussion of such goods see Fred Hirsch: *Social Limits to Growth* (Routledge and Kegan Paul 1977).
3   Hugh Raven, Tim Lang and Caroline Dumonteil: *Off our Trolleys?: Food Retailing and the Hypermarket Economy* (IPPR).
4   Charles Adams in *Common Sense in Advertising.*
5   *The Guardian* 18/10/91.

Chapter 8

Education

IF WE ARE to bridge the gap between the conventional economics of today and the ecological economics of the future, the building must be done by the people alive today and by our children and grandchildren. It is not going to be done by a *deus ex machina*, if only because there is no such thing. It is going to be done by you and me.

Looking round at each other, it may appear a mammoth task. But even among ourselves we can see signs of hope. And if we look at what is happening among the younger generation, our hope should grow.

Using the talents of humankind

But it will not be easy to effect the transformation and it means mobilising the talents of all, even those whom we have been used to writing off as useless or beyond redemption. Except for psychopaths no one is beyond conversion in this life, particularly by reality. ('I accept the world,' said Margaret Fuller, and Carlyle commented, 'Gad, she'd better!')

But it means, among other things, changing our system of education. Historically education has its roots in the natural process whereby children used to learn their living skills from the community into which they were born. It has changed under the industrial/capitalist system into a process whereby they are put into 'schools' which prepare them for jobs in an industrial economy.

As a result of this, our system in the West is geared to producing those whom the present economic system can most easily use and in most countries it follows the pattern of a puissance jumping competition in which the obstacles become progressively higher as you proceed round the course. In other words, instead of being a process of helping everyone to develop their varying talents, it is a process of elimination to ensure that only the lucky few survive who have those particular talents that the system wants.

And although the theory is that the system is geared to get the best out of everyone, in practice of course the conditions are so arranged that the lucky few are more than likely to be the children of those who are successful today. The Soviets had such a system to benefit the children of party members and it was much despised by all good democrats. Britain has such a system in the so-called public schools (as does WASP America with its preparatory schools) and it is tolerated and sometimes applauded even by those who would count themselves good democrats.

But our system has to be far more ambitious. To that end we need to try and learn from some of the more idealistic schemes of the past, although it is important that we also learn why they failed — if they did.

Valuing the unacademic

One of the most important things is to cherish gifts that are not 'academic'. There are two obvious traps into which we easily fall. One is in training our children to fill the employment vacancies of today (or, worse and more usually, of yesterday). That will always result in their skills being inadequate for the needs of tomorrow. The second trap is rather more subtle. We avoid the first trap and therefore plan to educate children in those skills which are most useful in helping them adapt to changing circumstances and to the different jobs which may emerge. This is the traditional method of training and selecting a civil service, so that the products do not have to know anything about agriculture to administer the Ministry of Agriculture (which can be painfully obvious). One snag here is that, while generalism is useful to everyone, it often fails to give experience of those disciplines which enable a generalist also to specialise. As a result our generalist in the Ministry of Agriculture may well underrate those with whom he or she comes in contact who actually know their subject. In the course of time he will swan off to the Home Office, leaving behind him an agricultural ministry firmly embarked on a wrong course. The other snag is that generalist skills tend to be of a particular academic kind, with the result that we therefore tend to neglect the development of any other skills.

The ideal philosophy is that held by a school like Millfield, which specialises in looking after the gifted in various fields but pays for itself (or used to) by taking rich dropouts and discovering their gifts. The underlying principle was that everyone has something at which they can become skilled.

This involves taking aboard the concept of 'multiple intelligences'. In his book of that name,[1] Howard Gardner lists seven distinct skills which he labels 'intelligences'. These are:

(1) musical;

(2) body-kinaesthetic or control of body movement (seen in sport and in all kinds of physical dexterity);

(3) logical-mathematical (problem-solving);

(4) linguistic;

(5) spatial (including a 'sense of direction');

(6) interpersonal intelligence (Gardner instances Anne Sullivan, the teacher

of the blind-deaf Helen Keller, as an outstanding example of someone with this intelligence);

(7) intrapersonal intelligence as displayed by those who are capable of a fruitful understanding of themselves. Gardner instances Virginia Woolf as a notable possessor of this intelligence and autistic children as obvious sufferers from a deficiency in this field.

To these I would add another:

(8) emotional/moral intelligence[2] which enables us to resist the temptations of the 'I Want it Now' mentality.

Now we could argue for ever as to whether 'intelligence' is the right word and as to how many of them there are. The ability to understand animals, for instance, is a gift which one might be tempted to regard as an extension of interpersonal intelligence, were it not for knowing people who have the former without a trace of the latter. Mary Midgeley has remarked, 'Wherever there are horses, some people prefer them to humans'. And I think we all recognise that there is this large range of gifts some of which are hardly touched by IQ tests or A Level exams.

These intelligences are far from mutually exclusive. Violin teachers, for instance, need a minimum of musical, body-kinaesthetic and interpersonal 'intelligences' to be really good at their job.

A civilised or sustainable education system needs to be able to recognise and help to develop these intelligences and the world, which is going to have more people than it has traditional jobs for, needs to value them. No civilisation is worthy of the name which has many people sick or emotionally handicapped and denies the job of caring for them to those who have the skills to do so but not the specialised ability needed to get an academic degree. No civilisation is worthy of the name which grants fortunes to those who are skilled at the adversarial rituals of the courtroom but which does not nurture the 'intelligences' of those who are natural interpersonal mediators (and most large families develop one of those among their number).

Why do we increasingly undervalue and underuse the abilities of those with intelligences 2, 3 and 5 who could with their repairing skills stop us becoming a 'throwaway society'?

A great deal of work has been done on how to educate these diverse intelligences by people like Sinichi Suzuki in the field of music and John Wilson[3] in that of 'moral education'.

Education in parenting

And possibly the most important education which is needed in the world is education in parenting. For anyone who sets any value on human beings will want succeeding generations to be brought up in such a way that they can both fulfil their own potential and look after the planet. However much is done in schools to help children, there is no substitute for the influence of parents, and particularly the mother, on the young child.

As a parish priest in a suburban parish I used to see many future fathers and mothers who came to make arrangements about their marriages. I have read accounts of clergy who manage to achieve a lot in 'preparation for marriage' and I believe some of them. Others I think are merely ways of saying that the authors refused to marry those of whom they did not personally approve.

In any case I found that, for complex and not very praiseworthy reasons, I was not myself good at doing anything about it — but since I could not help exercising my critical faculties on the situations before me, it was not difficult to identify the very few couples whose marriages, on the face of it, stood the slightest chance of lasting more than, say, ten years. And I think that the corollary of that judgement, if correct, was that the children of the others did not stand much chance of a satisfactory education for life. This, I should repeat, was in a 'respectable' area and those whom I saw were a self-selecting minority, being those who saw (or whose parents saw) some point in their being married in church (although often the only point was the glamour!)

What are we to do about that? How are we to break into the spiral of deprivation and start an upward spiral of successful education of successive generations?

The only possible course seems to be one of making it harder for people to have children. As I sat in the House of Lords in January 1996 listening to the House wrestling knowledgeably and humanely day after day with the question as to how one makes divorce laws work for the good of children, the question automatically appeared below the surface time after time, not 'how do we make divorce harder?' but 'how do we make marriage harder?' This becomes another of the basic questions which every ecologically aware citizen must face, and face it in a world where the emphasis is all on curing infertility even by drugs which produce multiple embryos.

Moral education and its egalitarian effects

Among the important ends of moral education (some would say the important end) is the imparting of *empathy*. Moral education is to do with learning how to deal with others and empathy is the not tremendously easy but not impossibly difficult task of imagining yourself in someone else's place so that you are able to extend the golden rule of 'not doing to others what you would not wish them to do to you' to a platinum rule of 'not doing to others what you would not wish done to you if you were them'. And this is, incidentally, the first step in obeying the Christian commandment[4] to love one another.

There are people who naturally have a gift for this (it is intelligence 6 in our list above) but most of us need training. A very few people are untrainable and those we call psychopaths.

Among other reasons for encouraging training in empathy is that it does not need much argument to demonstrate that if civilised democracies consisted of people who took that commandment seriously there would no longer be extremes of riches and poverty. It may not be all that easy to devise the political mechanisms to attain that. But, once given the will, it is not impossibly hard. As it is, it is quite obvious that the majority of the population is quite incapable of imagining themselves in the position of members of the underclass and that therefore they do not develop the will to do anything about the way society is organised.

Education in the Third World

When we look at deprivation in the Third World, we can use a number of measures.

People can be judged deprived in monetary terms. It is an important measure. But it can be pointed out (and not only by the comfortable who are of course the first to do so) that it is possible to be poor and happy. So we have learned to measure whether people's quality of life is 'deprived' rather than 'poor'. And to this the United Nations Development Programme has now added a measure of 'capability poverty'.[5] This is the measure as to whether people are able to grasp 'life chances' when they appear and a high rating is principally the result of investment in education and training.

But, of course, we are not talking about individuals only but about whole societies. To educate and train one person, particularly a female, is to a certain extent to educate and train future generations too.

---

1   *Multiple Intelligences* by Howard Gardner (Basic Books 1993).
2   Magnus Linklater and Giles Whittell: 'Why your child's EQ can matter more than IQ' in *The Times* 03/01/96.
3   Wilson, John: *Education in Religion and the Emotions; Practical Methods of Moral Education; Introduction to Moral Education; A Teacher's guide to Moral Education;* etc
4   This has a claim to be the only Christian commandment in that it is the only saying of Jesus of Nazareth which he calls a commandment. He was not given to ordering people about!
5   *Human Development Report 1996*, pp27 et seq.

Chapter 9

The need for sustainable development

Though the eradication of involuntary poverty remains a noble cause, the project of promoting maximal economic growth is, perhaps, the most vulgar ideal put before suffering humankind.

John Gray

WE LIVE IN an era when for the first time the educated citizen believes, rightly, that the medium-term prospect of human inhabitation of the earth is menaced by a wide variety of dangers.

The destruction of the ozone layer, global heating of the planet, problems posed by the depletion of non-renewable resources, over-population, desertification, the rape of the rainforests — ordinary intelligent citizens may not entirely believe that any one of these threatens them personally or immediately, but nevertheless they are aware that these factors *are* threatening their future and they would not care to lay heavy odds on their grandchildren not facing a greater and more immediate menace than anything they have encountered.

All this is relatively new. Our grandparents may have feared the Yellow Peril or a Martian invasion but they were confident that the first could be resisted by more Dreadnoughts and by British pluck — while the second was not a high probability. These were, as fears go, merely titillations.

But we are not titillated by lead in petrol or acid rain or organo-phosphate poisoning or a menace to our immune systems. We are scared, even if only mildly, by the products of progress. And we must recognise that this new phenomenon heralds a new era in the history of the world.

We know enough about the last ten thousand years or so to be able to plot a number of stages of 'development', but for the purposes of deciding what we need to do now, it should be sufficient to look at three of them: the agricultural revolution, the industrial revolution and the revolution which we are experiencing now, sometimes called the information revolution.

The agricultural revolution

The agricultural revolution in Britain enabled us to feed the growing population of an island before the development of long-distance bulk transport of food. Partly because of the English law of primogeniture, as opposed to the Roman law tradition of the mainland of Europe, this resulted in the increase of large land holdings and the consequent migration to the towns or the colonies of the rural population. And this made for what classical economists see as a much more efficient system of agriculture than that possessed by the peasant agricultural economies of the mainland. It also started the destruction of British rural society.

As always this was powered by greed. The enclosures have been well documented, not least by E. P. Thompson,[1] but the most well known example was the clearance of the Scottish highlands and islands by the landlords, often by the clan chiefs from whom protection was expected by the crofters because it was owed in the basic covenant of that society.

The settlers in the so-called New World started virtually from scratch with seemingly remote frontiers and without a peasant economy to begin with. The blocks of land allocated were already immensely large by European standards, and so settlers were able to move directly to an 'efficient' agriculture which then set a pattern for the rest of the world.

The industrial revolution and its effect on agriculture

The industrial revolution followed hard on the heels of the agricultural one and eventually even incorporated it. Agriculture ceased to be farming as it had been known since pastoral life began and became a series of production lines, of crops and of animals.

The small fields, which were small because they could be ploughed by one man with two horses in a day and manured by the same horses and the livestock on the same farm, were succeeded by prairies where rows of machines equipped with headlights churned on virtually 24 hours a day and the fertiliser was mined minerals or turned out by large chemical complexes. The small herds of cows and pigs known by name to the farmer and cunningly bred by experts with an eye for conformation and an instinctive gift for combining bloodlines were succeeded by large herds which could only be known by numbers, which were fed according to formulae, which were pumped full of chemicals, whose lifespan partly as a result was less than half of those of their dams, whose udders which they could hardly carry were milked by machine and who were killed in inhumane conditions on a production line.

Now this is about to be carried to its logical next stage by genetic engineering which will produce animals with specially improved organs whose ability to lead an ordinary animal life will be non-existent. As I revise this chapter in March 1997 the most prominent story in my newspaper is the development of a sheep in a laboratory from a single cell!

All this has been a natural corollary of the industrial revolution which brought the peasants in from the countryside to man the production lines, to work as long as possible on repetitious jobs which they did not have to understand, observed by men with stopwatches trying to see if they could be made to work harder.

If we could do this with industry, those who had become rich and powerful from it thought, why could we not do it with agriculture? It was true that the countryside was untidy and that one could re-educate people in towns rather more easily than animals in the countryside, but with application and money these drawbacks could be overcome. And many of them were.

Just as these two revolutions reached fulfilment in the West and were seeking to take over the rest of the world, along came the information revolution. Before we move on to consider this new phenomenon, let us take a look at some of the factors which powered the first two revolutions.

The growing importance of human capital and the decline of land and labour

The main factor in economics had become human-made capital. Land had ceased to be tremendously important. It was either virtually free as in the United States or it became more and more a mere commodity that you traded as in Europe.

Nor was labour any longer of major importance particularly since, with the arrival of fairly primitive technology, skills were not so much valued. Much greater skill was needed to cut and lay a hedge than to operate a mechanical hedge trimmer. Hence the riots of the much maligned Luddites who were protesting principally about the loss of their own livelihood but also, more fundamentally, about the loss of the value attached to skills. The change was not like that of the carriage to the car where the coachman might (or might not) become the chauffeur, and if the change came at the right time for a generation handover, the son of the coachman might become a mechanic.

In William Faulkner's *The Reivers*, Boon is employed as a member of the livery stable staff, since he has 'a way with horses and mules', but then the narrator's grandfather buys an automobile, not because he wants one but because his rival Colonel Sartoris has banned them from the town of Jefferson and the grandfather wishes to calmly and 'deliberately abrogate' the Colonel's decree. 'And Boon found his soul's lily maid, the virgin's love of his rough and innocent heart', and even Ned the coachman is seduced by the new beauty and the new skill. And they are able to marry the two by using the car to travel to an irregular horserace.

But with the looms and the cotton factories in England it was not as simple as that. The new machines needed less labour, though not at that stage stupefyingly less, and not enough skill to attract love and devotion.

But as labour and land became less important, human-made capital became more important. This caused all sorts of problems but none which was life-threatening until the second industrial revolution and the coming of the age of information technology.

Money market out of control

The arrival of information technology gave capital the freedom to roam the world looking for the places where money might best breed, which in effect meant finding those countries where the other factors of production, such as labour, were cheapest (or, as we put it in our quaint old-fashioned way, most badly paid); and it took full advantage of the opportunity. Many years ago I attended a Young Liberal Conference at Weston-super-Mare. It was for me a fairly unmemorable occasion, since before Jeffrey Archer (Lord Archer of Weston-super-Mare) the town's main claim to fame seemed to be that it had more fish and chip shops per head of population than any other town in the UK. But I heard there a memorable speech by Liberal MP Richard Wainwright. Richard is a Yorkshire Methodist layreader, a breeder of delphiniums; he is much liked and highly regarded by Liberals, and his main niche in history books will probably be that he could have been leader of the Liberal Party instead of Jeremy Thorpe if he had not declined to stand.

On this occasion Richard sketched a powerful image of capitalism. It was, he said, like a rogue elephant which had slipped the leg irons of civilisation and was roaming through the country, devouring what it could, trampling what it could not, leaving great heaps of stinking dung all over the place and constantly breaking down fences and seeking new tracts of country to wreck. I found it a potent image although it took some time before I fully understood how accurate it was.

We can now see this parable being acted out as the Trans National Corporations (TNCs), having exploited the land and labour of the 'developed' parts of our world, move on, leaving some stinking and poisonous dungheaps behind, to tap the virgin resources and cheap labour of the developing and undeveloped parts of the world.

On top of the movement of capital for 'productive' purposes, there is much movement which is purely speculative. Indeed John Eatwell, a Cambridge economist and now front bench spokesman on economics for Labour in the House of Lords, has estimated that 90% of the international movement of capital is for speculation.[2] One way of coping with this and one of the most urgent necessary steps is to exercise some control over the international movement of capital. The simplest method would probably be the 0.05% levy proposed by the UN Development Programme. But this idea was turned down by the 1995 G7 summit on the grounds that 'such a tax could impede international financial flows'.[3]

And while hankering after a golden past and lamenting a leaden present has been the hobby of every generation, previous generations have seldom been able to support their claims statistically. Thanks to the figures kept by the World Watch Institute, we are now able to see that the production of a large number of 'goods' per head of world population has started to decline for the first time in human history and that when Mr Macmillan told the citizens of the UK in the early sixties that they 'had never had it so good' he might, if he were addressing the population as a whole and not just Conservative voters, accurately have added: 'And nor will you ever again'.

The need for sustainable development

For a statesman to try to maximise GDP is about as sensible as for a composer of music to try to maximise the number of notes in a symphony.

The fact is that our Western civilisation has been hooked on quantity rather than quality. We in Europe have tended to think of this as an American vice from which we are elegantly free. But, in fact, it is an unavoidable disease of all those who measure life in terms of money and whose only measurements therefore are quantitative ones.

It is fair to say that the very best economic minds have always seen that the goal of mankind must be a steady state economy, which is anathema to capitalism. John Stuart Mill wrote: 'The increase in wealth is not boundless, at the end of the progressive state lies the stationary state. I cannot regard the stationary state of capital and wealth with the unaffected aversion so generally manifested towards it by political economists of the old school. I confess that I am not charmed with the ideal of life held out by those who think that the normal state of human beings is that of struggling to get on; that the trampling, crushing, elbowing, and treading on each other's heels which form the existing type of social life are anything but the disagreeable symptoms of one of the phases of industrial progress'. And Keynes agreed with him.

Finding ourselves in the situation we are in today and acknowledging a duty that we owe to our fellow men and women, as also to those who are (we hope) to follow after us, we are forced to acknowledge the need for sustainable development. 'Development' because the nature of humankind is such that we cannot be content to stay exactly where we are but must be always striving for something beyond ourselves, 'sustainable' because of our duty to future generations.

And for a definition of this key phrase 'sustainable development' I need go no further than the Brundtland definition: 'To ensure that development meets the needs of the present without compromising the ability of future generations to meet their own needs'. People being what they are, this definition has been endlessly queried, but I have not yet come upon an improvement, nor do I find that those who find it inadequate are doing more than nit-picking.

Or to put it rather more specifically: 'All projects should meet the following criteria. For renewable resources, the rate of harvest should not exceed the rate of regeneration (sustainable yield), and the waste of waste regeneration from projects should not exceed the assimilative capacity of the environment, and the depletion of the non-renewable resources should require comparable development of renewable substitutes for these resources'.[4]

Sustainable development demands that the pile-up of environmental 'bads' ends and that their production comes under control. And there are ills everywhere. We are all aware of the ills present in many of the Second and Third World countries but what of this description of one of the richest states of the richest country in the world?

Florida is getting a thousand new residents a day. The rivers and the swamps are dying. The whole state is being paved. There is enough money to make people rich but not enough to treat the sewage. The water supply is falling. Ordinary fishermen are an endangered species. Miami is the murder capital of the world. Droughts brown the landscape. People dare not go out at night.

Who needs deprivation if you can have riches like that?

Economic development: what is it?

Economic development is not merely another word for greed: it has worthwhile aims as well. It can increase the satisfaction or wellbeing of individuals; it can enhance and ensure certain freedoms, particularly freedom from ignorance, poverty and squalor; and it can nurture self-esteem, self-respect and independence.[5]

So we must embark on a path of finding a form of development which is qualitative and therefore sustainable.

1   'The spirit of agricultural improvements in the eighteenth century was impelled less by altruistic desires to banish ugly wastes or to feed a growing population than by desire for fatter rent-rolls and larger profits'. *The Making of the English Working Class*, p237.
2   Quoted by Noam Chomsky in *Resurgence*, 173.
3   Letter from Canadian Prime Minister Chrétien, 30/05/95.
4   Robert Constanza on p 113 of Gooland et al: *Population, Technology and Lifestyle*.
5   Pearce et al: *Blueprint for a Green Economy*, p30 et seq.

Chapter 10

The abolition of poverty

Behold the tears of the oppressed and they had no comforter; and on the side of the oppressors there was power but they had no comforter.

Ecclesiastes 4.1

THERE ARE MANY reasons why poverty should be combated wherever it is found and why every human being should share in the wealth of the planet. They vary from the ethically admirable to the purely practical. The former are often paraded but seldom acted upon. But what is really almost incomprehensible is that the practical reasons are so seldom even trotted out.

Maybe this is because when in 'moral mode' public figures do not like to get caught switching to 'practical mode'. But that cannot be the whole answer because in dealing with foreign affairs, politicians have no hesitation in switching from one to the other so swiftly that it is often difficult to pin down the true arguments that are being deployed.

Nevertheless it cannot be too firmly pointed out that the capitalist machine is a self-destructive one unless very tightly controlled. The history of capitalism over the last century, as we have seen, is that of reducing the need for labour. You can sell things more cheaply by paying the producers less. But if you take that to its logical conclusion or even some way along that path, you reach the stage where not enough people have the money to buy even the cheap goods that you have produced.

Keynesian economics realised this as a general proposition but still operated in a world where there was no great difficulty in finding markets if you 'primed the pump' sufficiently. But as the capitalist elephant charges across more and more frontiers trampling down what it discards (see Chapter 9) we can see a vista where there is increasing unemployment and therefore an increasing shortage of markets. It is therefore to the advantage of the capitalist machine to find some way of correcting this.

In order to do this it is necessary to look more closely at the nature of this unemployment; what then becomes immediately apparent is that there is no question of there not being enough work to do. It is the nature of the priorities of work that are changing, and the problem is that we have not found an economic mechanism for switching money into the new priorities.

The priorities forty and fifty years ago had to do with the production of goods. How were we to produce enough cars, dishwashers etc. to meet the demand, and when demand flagged how did we stimulate the demand in order to fuel the rogue elephant? Now there are more cars in the developed world than society can deal with and more people have washing machines than need them.[1]

The new priorities are obvious. We need teachers at a high ratio per pupil; we need nurses and experts in preventive medicine; we need an increasing number of people who will listen intelligently to their fellow human beings, to help those who find modern life difficult to pick their way through.

These are no new needs but they used to be met by the extended family and at one remove by the GP, the pastor and even on occasion by your friendly neighbourhood bobby. Now the cult of capitalist individualism has dispersed the extended family and overloaded the GP and the bobby. But if we are to have a civilisation we have got to put this together again, although it will inevitably take a different form. This involves recognising these roles as valuable and ensuring that those who perform them do not actually starve but can survive in modest comfort.

The importance of a cohesive society

A society in which this happened would be, to use the important terminology of Ralf Dahrendorf, an *inclusive* one[2] and certainly a cohesive one. Of course it would have to guard against the dangers which are involved in socialism (bureaucracy and over regimentation to start with) but it would cultivate the values of *conviviality* as Tony Crosland understood. Above all it would recognise the differing contributions of differing temperament types, as outlined for instance in the Myers-Briggs system,[3] and train people to work together in ways which respected each others' gifts and needs. The most obvious and simple example is the formation of teams which use the talents of both introverts and extroverts with understanding. That this may sound somewhat utopian shows just how far our educational system lags behind our understanding of both the theoretical and practical aspects of human potential.

That building such a society will need a massive transfer of money and a certain transfer of wealth over a period of time is undeniable but the difficulties of that have been wildly exaggerated, largely by those who would be at the dispensing side of the transfer. To put it at its crudest, Professor Peter Townsend calculated not all that long ago that 17.4% of income transferred from the top 20% of the population (in income terms) would double the incomes of the bottom 20%. The obvious commencing machinery for this is the Citizen's Income (also known as 'basic income') which would ensure a minimum income as of right for every citizen.[4] This is an idea which is already widely accepted. There appear to be two objections which have prevented it going further. One is the cost, and we have already noted (as has history *passim*) the unreadiness of the rich to shell out for others; the other is the suggestion that it creates an entitlement mentality instead of an obligation mentality. That comes richly from some of those who advance it but in the context of which I am writing it loses most of its validity in that a civilisation which is aware of the need for sustainability has by definition taught itself an obligation mentality anyway.

The inclusive society is one which will take seriously the needs of others. And the word 'needs' is used advisedly and strictly. It is not a question of gratifying people's desires, but of assuring them the possibility of leading lives as whole human beings.

'Needs' is a concept to be established at one end of a scale of desires and on such a scale it will take up a greater or larger portion depending on who is drawing the line;[5] a small portion of the scale will be taken up by ensuring that no one dies of starvation, a rather bigger one by assuring everyone the possibility of a modest social life or enjoyment of the four freedoms, and an even bigger one by accepting (within limits)[6] people's own estimates of their needs.

There is also a growing realisation that people do not live by bread alone and that 'needs' include, for all those above the starvation line, physical safety and even self-esteem (which means being valued for what we contribute and therefore entails the opportunity to contribute).

Apart from the ethical need to diminish inequality, there is the classical economic 'law of diminishing marginal utility' which says in effect that the more you have to spend the less utility it is to you. If I am hungry the expenditure of a pound on food will satisfy that hunger; if I start spending ten pounds, I am into satisfying my aesthetic longing for gorgonzola; if I spend a hundred I am probably into impressing a girlfriend. Therefore if we believe that we should be meeting the needs of the world at least cost, we will be in favour of allocating of the means of satisfying those needs as widely and therefore as cheaply as possible. Winnie the Pooh merely had to eat the contents of a pot of honey (giving himself great satisfaction) in order to have 'a useful pot for putting things in', a present for Eeyore produced at minimum cost, while Aspreys of Bond Street listed in a recent catalogue an item which, as far as utility goes, is described as a 'box' (presumably useful for putting things in) but which on account of the diamonds on it and the artistry of the design retailed at £485,000. Everyone needs boxes and jars but utility would be achieved for close on a million people by getting their containers from Pooh as opposed to one person getting his from Aspreys.

Poverty must be done away with, not in the sense that all the poor must be made rich but in the sense that both rich and poor must become wealthy.

We will consider later some of the more drastic measures which must be contemplated before we achieve that, but in the meantime there are some steps which must be taken which will start making the poor wealthy and which are necessary preconditions for them becoming so.

Partha Dasgupta, the distinguished Cambridge economist, has made out an unanswerable case for a basic need for 'civil liberties in the civil and political spheres, an effective legal judicial and regulatory system ... and the motivational forces necessary for the promotion of well-being, including a conscious attempt to separate the private and public sides of life'.[7] This is true wealth.

And tied up with poverty is, of course, unemployment. Indeed unemployment is not just a cause of poverty, *it is a form of poverty* since the need to work is universal. There is a psychological need to contribute something that is worthwhile. That something does not have to be what the world as a whole regards as worthwhile, nor does it have to be employment; the acknowledgement of one's peers that what one is trying to achieve is worthwhile will do. Prayer, rearing one's own children and making patterns with oil on canvas can all be deeply satisfying work.

But we now live in a world where the absence of worthwhile employment for a sizable portion of the human race is taken for granted. There is a culture of despair where the only possible hope is seen in chance, such as by winning the National Lottery.

We need to rediscover the virtue of work for its own sake. This involves reviving the professions, so brutally turned by Thatcherism into entrepreneurial firms, and trying to restore them to their rightful place in society. According to Ruskin there are five main professions: the soldier, the pastor; the physician, the lawyer and the merchant and they each have their own function in society and their own standards which they are prepared to die for rather than betray. The merchant's function is to provide for society. His function is not to make a profit for himself any more than the function of the clergyman is to get his stipend. And just as the duty of a captain is to be the last person to leave the ship in the case of wreck, so the manufacturer in any commercial crisis is bound to take the suffering of it with the staff.[8] Which would spell an end to the limited liability company.

Among the mail I received recently there was an advertisement for a boardgame called Gizzajob; 'following your chosen career path, the game takes you through the ups and downs of employment and unemployment as you answer questions, earn money and try to become the first player to achieve the Golden Handshake award. Can you make it to the top or will you go bankrupt?' You might say that all board games are equally cynical but at least in Monopoly you end up with a large number of useful buildings, not to mention a utility or two. But in Gizzajob the prize is nothing but money, a Golden Handshake being apparently the equivalent of Nirvana.

The problem of riches

And that really brings us to another question: Is the problem one of poverty or riches? Most people would unhesitatingly plump for the former. 'No one,' I heard a usually sensible academic woman say the other day, 'is against riches.' 'The dislike of riches always stems from envy,' a lifelong friend of mine (not rich himself) maintains.

But there is a small but significant lobby whose vote would go the other way. Among them we may discern not surprisingly the figure of Karl Marx. Let us not discount his testimony merely because his prescriptions have proved disastrous (like Adam Smith, Marx has many sins laid at his doors which are really those of less humane disciples). His diagnoses still reward examination.

Possibly less predictably a perusal of the reported teachings of Jesus of Nazareth reveals not a great emphasis on the poor ('They are always with us,' we are told) but a strong and almost virulent denunciation of riches and the rich. And Aristotle said: 'The greatest crimes are committed not for the sake of necessities, but for the sake of superfluities. Men do not become tyrants in order to avoid exposure to the cold'.[9]

But to turn to a less than household name (if he will forgive the description), the teacher C. Douglas Lummis: 'The problem of the problem of inequality lies not in poverty but in excess. This means that the solution to that problem is not a massive change in the culture of poverty so as to place it on the path of development; but a massive change in the culture of superfluity in order to place it on the path of counterdevelopment. It does not call for a new value system forcing the world's majority to feel shame at their traditionally moderate consumption habits, but for a new value system forcing the world's rich to see the shame and vulgarity of their over-consumption habits, and the double vulgarity of standing on other people's shoulders to achieve those consumption habits'.[10]

Why then hasn't there been a serious attack on poverty or riches? The answer comes back again to the fallacy of eternal growth. As long as growth continues or is thought to be going to continue, there is no great demand for an attack on poverty because everyone is shortly going to be better off than they were. But the realisation that this is not so will breed a situation where there will naturally come an attack on poverty. Which also involves, of course, an attack on riches.

Global income distribution is, not surprisingly, more horrifying than that even of the developed countries. The richest fifth of the world population receives 82.7% of total world income while the poorest fifth receives 1.4%.[11] Consider those figures with empathy!

Employment, labour and work

Everyone has a right to work under just and favourable conditions.
Article 23 of the Universal Declaration of Human Rights

Without work, all life goes rotten but when work is soulless life stifles and dies.

Albert Camus

'Man's power over nature should be used to shorten hours of work', wrote John Stuart Mill and a hundred years later the anticipated results have both surprised and shocked people.

They have been surprised that constant effort to reduce the amount of labour used in producing wealth has led to unemployment, and at least some of them have been shocked to find that the effects of this have been skewed so that a large number of people have no work and a few have far too much. The reason for their surprise is that they have fallen for the fallacy of infinite growth and believe that there will always be new jobs to replace the old. Of course there will, they admit, be frictional unemployment in the short term but that will be transitional and therefore unimportant! Even if they were right (and they are not) the lives and deaths of the human beings caught up in the transition are *not* unimportant.

But from the point of view of the economist and, as a result, from that of the employer, labour is an item of cost, to be replaced as quickly as possible by any cheaper item (such as capital goods) that may come along.

It may seem to any sane person, as it did to Bertrand Russell in 1935,[12] that if at a given moment you halve the amount of work which needs to be done to produce a million pins, the dividend is better taken in leisure by dividing the work between the workers than in cash. Yet the belief that the supply of jobs will be unending is so strong that this is never done.

Although the main reasons for unemployment in the modern world is the economic one I have mentioned above, one of the reasons that it is not tackled more radically is that everyone is ambivalent about toil.

Employment is valuable to all because it gives the employed money, a status and the impression (occasionally justified) that they are doing something useful. But the actual business of having to labour, whether in an office, a factory or a field, is burdensome. Roll on Friday!

Indeed, although they value employment, many people would like to spend as little time at it as possible, so that they can have time for their *real* work — which may be tending their garden, making their house a smart and efficient machine for living in (do-it-yourself), helping with the Scouts and Guides, or painting. 'I have so little time for my work,' a keen amateur (would-be professional) artist in well-paid office employment said to me once.

So what is the nature of the true work of Man? In *Small is Beautiful* Schumacher lays before us the threefold functions of work under Buddhist economics. (We can forget if we want to the Buddhist part. He cast his remarks in that way because they were originally part of a series of lectures in Asia: in fact the description would apply to almost any theory of work produced in an ethical framework which takes humanity seriously.)

The threefold functions are: to give each person a chance to utilise and develop their faculties; to enable them to overcome their egocentredness by joining with other people in a common task; and to bring forth the goods and services needed for a becoming existence.

Measured by these standards the traditional Scottish shepherd, with a degree from St Andrew's and sitting on a hillside among his sheep reading Plato in the original, does better than most merchant bankers. There may or may not have been an actual example of this figure but we must wish that there had been.

The use and abuse of technology

If this is what we need work for, then the way in which we should be using technology becomes clearer and we must, incidentally, be sure that we are using technology and not just allowing technology to use us.

The primary use of technology is to lighten the burden of work we have to carry in order to stay alive and develop our potential. I am using my computer at the moment to enable me to finish a book which I hope will be helpful to my fellows (and which seems to me at the present time the fulfilment of my faculties!). Without it the book would, I have no doubt, be worse and take longer — if it ever got completed at all. Perhaps if Dr Casaubon in George Eliot's *Middlemarch* had had a computer, his *Key to all Mythologies* would have been completed and the world would have been better informed for a bit (and maybe even wiser).

One of the main uses of technology is to enable people to work where they want to, to have their place of employment near to both their homes and their leisure activity. This cuts down the time they have to spend in travel and incidentally may mean that the travelling they do is safer. According to the California Highway Patrol, among the activities undertaken by drivers while travelling at close on 70mph are taking out their contact lenses, taking off their bra, feeding their baby, changing its nappy, and cutting its hair. And some people are worried about the increased risk of accidents when working at home!

1   A mechanical dishwasher is needed virtually all the time by a family with children; for the retired and the young, the job is more efficiently done in the old fashioned way with a sink and a drying up cloth tastefully printed with the Tower of London plus a stimulating conversation about the nature of the universe (or the prospects of Leeds United) between Washer and Drier.

2   Ralf Dahrendorf et al: *Wealth Creation and Social Cohesion*, p34 et seq.

3   Isabel Briggs Myers and Peter Myers: *Gifts Differing*.

4   Prof James Meade: *Full Employment Regained* (Cambridge University Press 1995).

5   Adam Smith himself put it well: 'By necessities I understand not only the commodities which are indispensably necessary for the support of life, but whatever the custom of the country renders it indecent for creditable people, even in the lowest order, to be without'.

6   'Dammit,' exclaimed the eighteenth century nobleman when it was suggested to him that he might start retrenching his establishment by sacking his pastrycook, 'a feller must have his biscuit!'.

7   Partha Dasgupta: *An Inquiry into Well-being and Destitution*.

8   John Ruskin: *Unto this Last* (Essay 1).

9   Aristotle: *Politics* 1267a.

10   C. Douglas Lummis: 'Equality' in *The Development Dictionary*, ed Wolfgang Sachs.

11   UNDP: *Human Development Report 1992*.

12   Bertrand Russell: *In Praise of Idleness and Other Essays* (London: Allen and Unwin 1935).

Chapter 11

Loyalties and functions in politics and economics

W E, TOGETHER WITH our immediate forebears who produced the climate of opinion in which we were brought up, have lived through a period starting with the 'enlightenment' in which many people think that the human race has reached its fulfilment through the promotion of the individual as the most important unit of humanity. The climax of this train of thought was possibly marked by the moment when the prime minister of Britain could say, 'There is no such thing as society. There are only individuals.' Since then the pendulum has started to swing slowly back to a situation where we see that individuals can only fulfil themselves when they are part of a community and that communities and their lives are taken as seriously as the life of the individual.

For intelligent people have always known that if you start sacrificing all to the individual, it in effect means sacrificing all to 'me', since I am the most important individual I know. Complete selfishness creates an intolerable society in which the overwhelming majority of people will be both poor and miserable. Nor is there much satisfaction for anybody in going to the other extreme and sacrificing all for Gaia or the universe. Rather, human society has put itself together over the ages in such a way that there are appropriate levels of co-operation between people for almost all activities — from the choice of works of art by the individual (*chacun à son goût*) right up to the necessity for global peacekeeping which can only be done at a supranational or (just possibly) a regional level.

The importance of natural communities

In the complexities of today's life there is always a tendency towards centralisation. The most obvious and the most criticised example lies in the recent command economies of Marxism and it is worth noting that the real economic failure here (as opposed to the political ones) was that they flourished too soon in the history of the world, before civilisation had furnished them with the technological machinery to enable them to do their job efficiently. For if you are not to have a revolution you must satisfy at least some of the real wants of people as well as providing them with what you believe to be their needs, and it is impossible to satisfy the wants of people unless you know what they are. If you try and guess those wants you always guess wrong, for the same reason that (as we saw in Chapter 8) educational planners are always training people for the career needs of a previous generation and generals are proverbially always solving the questions posed by the previous war. Life moves too fast for all but the most empathetic of planners.

It is ironic that the people living under these command economies finally revolted at the moment when those economies could have been made to work. The development of computers and electronic communication means that it would now be possible for a centrally directed economy to find out what people want. But it probably would not have done the Soviet Union any good to have learned this, since the desirability of running the economic system in that way would have clashed with the political undesirability (as far as its leaders were concerned) of giving people access to telephones and photocopiers, both as much tools of insurrection as pitchforks and torches were in an earlier age.

Although the Marxist command economies are the most obvious examples of centralisation, there are sufficient other examples to show that there is a natural centripetal tendency at work. Americans are always having to fight to preserve the reality of a federal system which retains serious rights for the individual states. Even in tiny Britain a Conservative Party which was originally elected partly by promising to break up the power of the state and return it to the people ended up as a greater centralising power than any socialist government which believed in centralisation had ever been, virtually destroying the countervailing power of local government and creating instead quango (Quasi Autonomous Non Governmental Organisation) after quango of unelected appointed nominees of central government.

The mistake that the British Conservative Party made in this last case was to think that when you are wielding power it must always be exercised either centrally or by individuals. If that is the choice, the truth is that central government will always (whatever its ideological beliefs) choose that it itself must exercise the power (because it is elected 'to govern' and the individual might choose differently and therefore wrongly and 'against the wishes of the national electorate'). The only system which is efficiently democratic is one which has different levels of power representing different levels of community (federal and state or national, regional and local) which can trade off the interests they represent against the interests of the next tier up, although it is usually considered (chiefly by the highest rung of authorities) that the system must work in such a way that in a crunch the highest rung of authority prevails. A classic example of this is when the national electorate is deemed to have decided that it needs nuclear power but no local community wishes to have a nuclear power station. This is usually regarded as NIMBYism (Not In My Back Yard) and it is assumed that the national interest must prevail. Such a situation will clearly result in more and more power going central as government acts to save time and trouble by seeing that such disputes do not arise.

The solution to this problem which most countries have arrived at is to have a written constitution which outlines the powers which each tier possesses. Britain is one of the very few countries not to have such a constitution and it is for this reason that, as often as not, any solution it finds to problems about the appropriate level of decision making is at the end of a centripetal path.

Apart from the basic UK problem of no constitution an almost equally harmful factor is that everyone tends to use the language of 'devolution' as if power naturally belonged at the top and those who held it should be persuaded, of their great kindness, to let some 'trickle down'. But in a democracy power by definition belongs to the people and what needs to be done is not to force power down from above but to remove the hindrances to people governing themselves at the local level. True devolution is not shoving power down. Rather it is ensuring that the rights of those on the lower rungs of the organisational ladder to govern themselves are preserved.

This involves both a significant tax-gathering power at the most local level, and local organisations training themselves in valuing voluntarism which includes among other things the celebration of the gifts of the volunteers — as happens, for instance, in Finland.[1]

If the basic level of the exercise of power is the local community then it must be a genuine local community, not an artificial one. For instance the present London boroughs are three times as big as they should be and although I in Clapham know that I am in the London Borough of Lambeth, I do not feel any connection with that entity; I have no desire to dance the Lambeth Walk on high days and holidays, much as I enjoyed doing so when young. On the other hand I do identify with the 'man on the Clapham omnibus' who is the archetypal sensible man and with the Clapham Sect who brought about the Abolition of Slavery. The original local boroughs of the 1950s did represent communities, as G. K. Chesterton recognised in *The Napoleon of Notting Hill*. In that important and prophetic novel the King reinstates the boroughs 'in their ancient magnificence. Each borough shall immediately build a city wall with gates to be closed at sunset. Each shall have a city guard armed to the teeth. Each shall have a banner, a coat-of-arms and, if convenient, a gathering cry.' And then in the book the usual thing happens (it might be the 1990s): commercial interests want to run a road through several boroughs. One borough objects; and war follows.[2]

And the moral of that is *not* that power should not be entrusted to local units but that there are certain matters, such as war and peace, and for that matter human rights, for which the appropriate level of decisions is at a higher level, while in less fundamental matters it is right that people should have power over their daily lives. No matter what the arguments may be for economies of scale, real or imagined, local government will only work satisfactorily if it is built with the bricks of real local loyalties of *village* dimensions.

In our great conglomerate society it is not always easy for the bureaucratic mind to identify villages. Just occasionally, of course, they are obvious. I lived for five years in the London suburb of Kew. It was easy enough to see that we were a village. We were bounded by two main roads (which for once defined rather than slashed us) and by the River Thames and I think most of us felt affronted that the Post Office insisted we put 'Richmond, Surrey', instead of 'Kew, Surrey' as our postal address. But although other villages are not so obviously defined, the individual usually identifies with one such area and, as always, it is the local people who should decide.

Above the village the next really serious level of organisation is that of the nation. To say this is not to disparage the importance of (say) the English counties, merely to suggest that the intermediate tiers between true local communities and the nation are both debatable and optional. There almost certainly should be at least one such intermediate tier. I feel myself a citizen of Clapham, as also of London, of England (though not, myself, of the UK), Western Europe (Christendom) and the world. I wish to be represented in the government of Clapham and I wish Clapham to be represented in the government of London. At this intermediate stage it should be noted that the representation becomes indirect. And that is probably right. But it becomes direct again as I register my wish to have a say in the direction (in both senses of the word) of the nation to which I belong. But since I am not a Welshman, a Scot or an Irishman I have no desire to tell them how to run their own affairs.

But my next home on the ladder is Western Europe. I am a product of a civilisation based on Greece and Rome and inspired by the Western churches. And in that fellowship I wish to find myself allied to Wales and France, to Scotland and Germany, to Ireland and Italy (but not to Turkey).

And finally I realise (and feel) that all people are siblings and that in the world in which I live there is now a lot which can only be done by the nations (or blocs) getting together and acting in concert in a global body.

Now my choice of loyalties may not be everyone's (although I would bet on wide agreement up to national level) but my case is that we should find out what the levels are on which most people agree and then put into practice a system of governance based on them. This is much better than allocating power without consulting people as to their real loyalties, as at present, which wastes an enormous amount of time, effort and money as various bright ideas are put into practice and then scrapped.

> Free Trade must now be indicted for having ravaged the environment; laid waste ... traditional manufacturing industries and communities in the West; spawned horrific proletariats of displaced persons in industrial conurbations ... and created a financial tyranny.
>
> Peter Cruttwell: *Industry out of Control*

Administering power: the argument for blocs

Above the nation state there is clearly room for considerable argument as to the appropriate levels of governance in a world committed to sustainable development. Sustainable development means living within environmental constraints of regenerative and absorptive capacities. We must not produce what we cannot dispose of without damage to the environment; nor must we consume that which we cannot replace without damage to the environment. For example we (and those with whom we share the administration of such matters) must not catch more fish than can reproduce themselves 'naturally', unless we can breed more without depleting fossil fuels or the ozone layer, without causing harm to stock by weakening their resistance to disease, or causing harm to the consumers. Given a certain balance which nature seems to have imposed, this demands a rigorous application of the precautionary principle. We are not to assume that because we can produce some more productive form of fish or animal for one generation or so without immediately obvious ill-effects, that we can immediately start production on a large scale without the most rigorous testing for all possible side effects.

There are three scales on which it is theoretically possible to police such an approach effectively. The first is the global scale but this is purely theoretical in that it is obvious to all that our global machinery has not yet become more than marginally capable of the task involved. Nevertheless we should persevere at this level since eventually it is only on the global scale that we will be able to control the TNCs.

The second possible level for policing is the nation. This unit has the advantage that it has over a long period of time worked out institutions and traditions of collective action, responsibility and mutual help. Its disadvantages are that most nations are probably not complex enough to be self-supporting and are seldom capable of controlling TNCs.

The third possible scale is that of a group of nations with roughly the same cultural and economic background, such as Western Europe. But, as with the London boroughs, one must not construct an administrative unit which satisfies only administrative or monetary criteria. Any such grouping, if it is to work, must have emotional ties as well. It is for this reason that I am personally extremely dubious about plans to expand the European Union further. Turkey is clearly not culturally a part of Europe. The Russian culture is completely different from that of the West and possibly that applies to all countries whose basic religion is Christianity in its 'Orthodox' form.

But it is also important that the bloc should be economically if not homogeneous at least compatible. Each economic unit keeps healthy by allowing its richer (and usually more central) areas to subsidise its poorer (and usually more outlying) areas. In the UK the Home Counties subsidise the Welsh hill areas; in the EU Germany, France and the UK subsidise Greece and Portugal. The larger your unit the bigger the political difficulty of persuading the rich to subsidise the poor. You can just about persuade the Germans to subsidise their fellow nationals in the East but it will be far more difficult to persuade Ireland to subsidise Bulgaria.

So the second area (the natural community being the first) which needs careful consideration in the sustainable world is the 'bloc' or federation of countries. There is one major example in the world today (the European Union) and a number of embryo or potential ones — such as the North American Free Trade Area (NAFTA).

There are a number of arguments for these. For instance the European Union was put together with the admirable aim that there should never again be war in Western Europe. But another possible advantage is that members can help countries which are over-extended to share their burdens. For instance it is difficult to see how over-populated England could have a sustainable economy, but possible to see how Western Europe could carry England while the latter takes steps to reduce its population over a period of time and possibly has other gifts to contribute.

It is tempting to suggest that the obvious unit for Britons is the UK but the drastic over-population of England makes this not very attractive, while a unit consisting of Western Europe makes both cultural and economic sense. But it does carry with it the need to make the European Union an effective and democratically controlled unit. A confederation of governments such as that of North America or the European Union still has enough power to control TNCs which are now more powerful than many individual nations on their own. TNCs need to be subjected to international regulation. Ideally this would (and will eventually) be done by the UN but any attempt to do so to date has been blocked by those countries in which the TNCs are most powerful (the US, the UK etc.) and who blocked even the mention of the problem in the GATT negotiations and at Rio.

It may well be asked how, if the developed countries are those that at present block global action, they are to be persuaded to initiate bloc action; but there is a marked psychological difference between exercising your own sovereignty (in concert with allies with whom you have a basic sympathy) against corporations operating within your sphere, which would be the case in the EU, and our present situation of being asked by a global body, with which we do not feel much solidarity, to force traders who may be based in our own country to refrain from despoiling other countries whom we have grown used to despoiling ourselves over a long period of time. Sad but true! But we will never achieve sustainable development unless we force TNCs to internalise in their prices the full environmental and other costs of their activities. These would include rehabilitation and replacement (possibly by means of internationally controlled performance bonds), clean-up, fair wages, and other factors.

If a bloc (say Western Europe) has rules to enforce these matters within its own boundaries — and it should be emphasised that such a regime would satisfy both the two major political-economic philosophies of our times in that it is compatible both with socialism and also with any really viable theory of privatisation — it will be much more sympathetic to helping another weaker bloc (say Africa) to do the same. Thus we will build stepping stones from the nation state towards world government.

Perhaps it is at this level (since experience shows that the World Bank is powerless or without motivation in this matter) that constraint can be imposed on national indebtedness which at all levels from the US down to the more obviously poor nations leads to major ills (including eventually, almost inevitably, inflation). If a nation owes enormous amounts of money which it cannot pay except in the very long term, it either starts to print money or it has to get rid of democratic government in order to retrench (or both).

One way of imposing restraint is by way of bloc central Banks. The Group of Green Economists[3] disapproves of central banks because they are not subject to democratic control but I believe that central banks are acceptable provided that the tasks that they are given are limited. There are certain jobs which democracy is not qualified to administer because the short-term temptations involved in their administration are too great. One of these is world peace, another is the administration of justice; yet another is the control of inflation. But to say this is not to deny that there must be ultimate democratic control; it is merely to say that such control must be exercised at one remove. In each case it is the job of democracy to set up the machinery, while not itself controlling the administration of the system once the machinery is set up. Control of inflation is a fundamental need and, as in New Zealand, the task of implementing it can be given to a central bank hedged round with safe-guards.

The fundamental flaw in the philosophy of free trade is that it assumes immobility of capital between nations. Where that does not exist, as in the modern world, the whole theoretical justification of free trade collapses. It may well be impossible, and it may even be undesirable (though I doubt it), to go back to international immobility of capital, nevertheless blocs will feel the necessity to exercise some controls over capital movement if only to ensure a taxation base.

It may be that it will be easier for blocs than for nations to start the long hard road of limiting the ecological footprints of the developed countries. Professor R. H. Tawney remarked that rich people are 'a small class which wears several men's clothes, eats several men's dinners, occupies several families' houses and lives several men's lives'.[4] We are beginning to see that this is true of rich countries too. Dutch economists have calculated that for each hectare of their own country a Dutch citizen 'uses', they 'use' five hectares outside, mainly in the Third World. And if that is true of the Netherlands how big is the footprint of the USA? The slimming process will not be easy but it may be slightly easier if neighbours are all doing it together.

Blocs as civilisations

We have recently had our attention drawn to the global importance of civilisations.[5] This again is something that I think most of us know in our bones. It may be expressed tritely as in 'East is East and West is West and never the twain shall meet' or it may come out almost subliminally as in 'the real reason' why Turkey will never be admitted to the European Union, which the Turkish President has said is 'that we are Muslim and they are Christian [but] they [the EU] won't say that'.

The importance of cultures reveals itself obviously to the rest of the world in the double standards the West shows in its differing treatment of Iran and Serbia. A world of clashing civilisations is inevitably a world of double standards: people apply one standard to their kin-countries and a different standard to others.

The formation of civilisation blocs is a natural development which many people have long foreseen. Looking back over history we have experienced the usurpation of the 'family' by the 'tribe' and the 'tribe' by the 'nation' and we are now seeing in our own time the emergence of bigger units. Some have thought, on the evidence of worldwide instant communication and the growth in power of the TNCs, that we would move directly from nation states to world government — but that is clearly too quick a jump. It looks as if a very dangerous period of 'civilisation blocs' lies ahead. It is particularly dangerous because the domination of the world by the 'non-Orthodox Christian' West has been too much that of a colonial power. How long will the world put up with a situation where 15% of the population dominate the remaining 85%? And the danger of and to the West becomes more obvious as its nations try to defy the economic laws of gravity and as their internal civilisation dissolves. Budgetary discipline in the West is disappearing and law and order is collapsing. Since 1960 the US population has increased by 41% while violent crime has risen by 560%.[6]

World governance

War and blackmail

There will be a need for global organisation if only to keep world peace. Blocs should be able to do that within their own boundaries (after all it was the original *raison d'être* of the European Union) but there is always the danger of inter-bloc strife[7] to be guarded against and a global society will need a global parliament such as the UN. And the keeping of world peace will also mean steps for policing world blackmail. The mad scientist who holds the world to ransom has been the staple of thrillers for over a hundred years but now he shows signs of becoming a reality. Dr Karl Johnson is quoted in *The Coming Plague* as saying; 'It is only a matter of months — years, at most — before people nail down the genes for virulence and airborne transmission in influenza, Ebola, Lassa, you name it. And then any crackpot with a few thousand dollars' worth of equipment and a college biology education under his belt could manufacture bugs which would make Ebola look like a walk around the park.'

The World Bank and others

There is a large range of (on the whole, harmful) world governance already in place operating through the World Bank and other organisations. It tends to be harmful because it is (a) governed by old-style economics and (b) uncontrolled by democracy. In their structural adjustment programmes the IMF have had a picture of an ideal country which corresponds to no known place on earth. In almost all cases, adjustment has required deflationary policies and cutbacks in welfare services which result in hardship for the poor while the elites who have access to foreign exchange have done very well. The environment and communal solidarity also suffer as a result of the intensive cultivation of cash crops needed to solve the problem of trade balances.[8]

Ecological control

We must be wary of giving a global authority too much to do, given that as democrats we wish to keep power as near to the people as possible and bearing in mind the record of the World Bank, but we are in a situation where the ecological problems of the world pose as great a threat as the nuclear bomb and probably, like it, have to be controlled on a global scale.

Chancellor Kohl of Germany has suggested a Global Environmental Council along the lines of the UN Security Council. Although the idea has not received much support it may well be that the next successor conference to Rio, meeting in a situation of increased ecological threats, may produce something along those lines. There are areas where a global body may have to challenge what have hitherto been regarded as 'legitimate national interests'. Kennedy Graham has queried whether it is a legitimate interest for Americans to consume 26,000 tons of coal-equivalent per head annually (compared with Germany's 13,000 and Ethiopians 55), or for Australians to eat 800kg of cereals while Africans eat 65, or for countries to be encouraging a higher population growth (as Bulgaria, France, Iraq, Israel and Saudi Arabia have recently done).[9]

It is at the global level too that we can most effectively control TNCs...

Control of the TNCs

Your corporate types are soon going to be a stateless superclass, people who live for deals and golf dates and care a lot more about where you got your MBA than the country you were raised in. It's the Middle Ages all over again, these little unaffiliated duchies and fiefdoms, flying their own flags and ready to take in any vassal who will pledge his life to the manor. Everybody busy patting himself on the back because the Reds went in the dumper is going to be wondering who won when Coca-Cola applies for a seat in the UN.   Scott Turow in *Pleading Guilty*

Needless to say it hasn't been easy to create an economic system able to produce 358 billionaires while keeping another 1.3 billion people in absolute deprivation. It took long and dedicated effort by legions of economists, lawyers and politicians on the payrolls of monied interests to design and implement such a system.

David Korten writing in *Resurgence*

To attract companies like yours... we have felled mountains, razed jungles, filled swamps, moved rivers, relocated towns... all to make it easier for you and your business to do business here.

Philippine Government advertisement in *Fortune Magazine*.

The new players in world affairs are the TNCs and the NGOs. The world's 300 largest industrial corporations own some 25% of the world's productive assets. Of the world's hundred largest 'economies' half are now not nations but TNCs .[10] TNCs (which are different from multinationals in that the latter conduct their subsidiary businesses entirely in the counties they colonise whereas TNCs buy labour abroad to sell in the developed countries) can of course behave constructively but their natural instinct is that of uncontrolled and unreformed capitalism. David Korten tells the story of the Pacific Lumber Company which pioneered the development of sustainable logging and had a humane but costly employment policy. 'This made it a prime takeover target'. Sure enough it was taken over, its logging policy changed to maximise immediate returns, its pension fund was raided and the proceeds invested in junk bonds which went broke. The really big and dedicated TNCs concentrate on persuading countries or states (within federations) to give them tax-free deals in order to come and invest. Global competition is about local communities and workers competing against one another to absorb ever more of the production costs of the world's most powerful and profitable organisations.[10] The fact is that in any country there are two parallel economies with conflicting interests: the corporate economy and the national economy. Corporate profits rise as personal earnings and employment fall.

And the appetites of the TNC's are insatiable At the moment they are hovering like vultures around China where the annual television advertising spend is projected to rise to £7 billion by 2005! And their morals (and grammar) are non-existent. 'We want to put soft drinks within arm's reach of desire ... and schools are one channel we want to make them available in,' Randal W. Donaldson, spokesman for Coca-Cola in Atlanta, is reported as saying. Dr Reggie von Zugbach of the Glasgow Business School put the attitude to ethics in a nutshell in a letter to *The Times* when he said: 'If the Fayeds lied to the Department of Trade and Industry officials, breaking no law, this must be judged as the normal and proper behaviour of competent and responsible entrepreneurs'.

Like all large and powerful bodies the TNCs coin their own language. Efficiency means employing fewer people, not that the same people are working better. The term free trade is used as if it meant freedom for people to choose how they want their world to be run, instead of meaning, as it does, freedom for the corporations to pursue profitability ruthlessly.

Quite what rights corporations have or should have is a complex question. It is likely that in a sustainable economy there is no room for the limited liability company, which is an ingenious invention to enable people to borrow money on the strength of an uncertain future and not be responsible for paying it back if their expectations are not fulfilled.

In the meantime there are a great many ways in which TNCs can be restrained and made to pay their way: these include taxes on financial instruments of all kinds, and especially on currency trading; heavy surtax on capital gains to make speculation unprofitable; and a granting of the right of communities and workforces to buy out a business or part of a business which is being closed.

Another constructive step would be to limit the protection of 'intellectual property'. This should be defined and interpreted narrowly and granted only for the minimum period of time necessary to allow those who invest in research to recover their costs and a reasonable profit.

As it is, the strong attempts to extend patent protection over genetic materials on the ground that they will speed the advance of agricultural research and improve global food security is a blatant effort by a few corporations to establish monopoly control over the common biological heritage of the planet. It is time too to put a curb on advertising. This consumes the efforts of some of the cleverest (though by definition not the wisest) brains in the community to persuade the rich that they want products which they clearly do not need. The world can clearly not afford that. It is not difficult to distinguish between the giving of necessary information to the public, and such persuasion. But for the time being, anyway, TNCs are with us and can and must be controlled and used in the interests of the planet. For instance Costa Rica's National Institute of Biodiversity has done a deal with the pharmaceutical company Merck whereby the latter funds a conservation and research programme in return for access to the results, and if there is a commercial result the Institute gets royalties.

But TNCs must eventually be controlled at global level — partly because, as we have seen, some of them are economically bigger than nations, but also because it is world governance organisations like GATT and WTO which give TNCs their freedom and which must be reformed if TNCs are going to be controlled. It is true that human beings have been fighting back on the local level. A small largely Hispanic community in Houston, Texas which took on one of the largest chemical companies in the country negotiated an agreement to institute citizens' audits of the pollution control equipment. This citizen review process has been written into the company's permit to operate in Texas.[11] Likewise California has taken a brave step forward in taxing TNCs on the estimated accounts of what they actually do in that state, although it is in danger of being overruled at national or international level. And these efforts have only succeeded because the companies concerned have not deployed their biggest weapon: emigration.

Cargill, the world's greatest grain trader, has been temporarily halted in both Japan and India. In Japan the grain trading houses (the Zaibatsu) launched a campaign against allowing Cargill in on their game and because they had the government on their side managed to delay them. In India the peasants have resisted Cargill, partly by demolishing a seed factory by force.[13]

But these are probably merely rearguard actions and TNCs are able political operators. At Rio they effectively blocked recommendations and even discussions about their operations. A voluntary code of conduct drawn up by the Business Council on Sustainable Development (a corporate lobbying group) was substituted for the recommendations of the UN's Centre for Transnational Corporations which were not even circulated. A few months later the Centre itself was quietly shut down.

The obvious machinery for international effort lies in the UN, although it is only since its system was originally built that environmental security has emerged as a third pillar of international relations along with military and economic security. It is sometimes held that there is already a *de facto* world government in the shape of the World Bank, the IMF, GATT, the World Trade Organisation (WTO), the G7 Executive and so on. Some of these bodies already wield immense power. Many people argue that the World Bank is basically an institution for creating and increasing international debt — that is its metier, but in the process of doing so it must be regarded as a governance institution, exercising power through its financial leverage to legislate entire legal regimes and even to alter the constitutional structure of borrowing nations. Bank-approved consultants often rewrite a country's trade policy, fiscal policies, civil service requirements, labor laws, health care arrangements, environmental regulations, energy policy, resettlement requirements, procurement rules, and budgetary policy.

Para 4 of Article XVI of the GATT agreement setting up the WTO stipulates that: 'Each member shall ensure the conformity of its laws, regulations and administrative procedures with its obligations as provided in the Annexed Agreements' (which may well restrict the ecological protection countries can give their citizens. The presumption is always in favour of more trade!) Much of this power should be abolished on the way to more democratic control but if there is an area for giving a global organisation more authority it is in the realm of those matters which affect the whole human race far into the future — though even here, of course, there should be some eventual democratic control. But there are already signs that there is a demand for greater and different responsibilities to be exercised, even if the will to pay for them is not all that apparent.

President Clinton has called on the UN to fight international drug traffic and with the international mobility of money has come the international mobility of criminals such as Nick Leeson of Barings and Syed Ziauddin Ali Akbar of the Bank of Credit and Commerce International.

Another partially achieved step forward is in the Framework Convention on Climate Change 1992. Other areas more or less tackled include outer space (virtually not); the electromagnetic spectrum and geostationary orbits; Antarctica; whaling; coastal fisheries and offshore oil.

Yet another area for global co-operation could be the establishment of international stockpiles of critical commodities such as oil to meet worldwide shortages (real or contrived) with agreed criteria for releasing them.

As to what form such a UN ecological oversight should take, there is much argument. Among the runners are a Global Environmental Organisation, an Environmental Security Council (a suggestion from the UK among others), or a switch of purpose for the existing Trusteeship Council — but there is doubt (as always) about the funding, particularly since very limited resources were provided for the Global Environment Facility (GEF) which is regarded in some quarters as a prototype.

One way forward would be for the World Bank and the IMF to be persuaded that environmental reform should be an element in restructuring. And the WTO is charged with exploring ways to ensure that trade rules and environmental goals are 'mutually supportive'.

None of these will be at all easy. Mexico has successfully argued before a GATT panel that a US initiative to protect dolphins was illegal and the EU has argued (though unsuccessfully) that US laws designed to promote the purchase of fuel efficient vehicles are a trade barrier. In addition these bodies are notably opaque and undemocratic. Cases are heard behind closed doors by panels of bureaucrats and lawyers and there are few opportunities for citizen groups to submit their points of view.

Control of 'footprints'

At a level which will start as a national one as countries begin to realise the international implications of ecological responsibility (as the Netherlands and Denmark are already doing), but which will eventually have to become international when enough nations have seen the light, is the question of national 'footprints'; we have to take a fresh look at our use of ecological space to ensure that we in the developed world are not stealing the assets of poorer countries.

Just as Britain's ecological footprint sixty years ago covered the whole of the Empire (over a third of my schoolroom globe was coloured red) because its political footprint was the same, so today the area Europe affects through trade and other relationships in order to remain richer than other countries is, according to Friends of the Earth, 50% larger than it should be in a world of sustainable development. It is worth pointing out that increasing the footprint is called becoming more competitive and is still accounted a virtue. We will have to change this way of thinking if we are to survive.

At a lower level bilateral agreements can be helpful. An example is the agreement by Sweden to pay for the installation of emission control equipment in Poland, whose emissions affect Sweden.

It is important to note that where nations actually share responsibility for goods which they own and are protecting them (e.g. rivers which flow through their countries) agreements tend towards the highest common denominator, whereas where they assume burdens for the protection of sinks for which they have no feeling of ownership (e.g. the Atlantic) they drift towards the lowest.

But... communities

But the major pressure for progress may be found in the need to work at a very local level. Local government, especially if elected democratically (proportionally), can be immensely effective in organising information feedback which will change people's attitudes — for instance in the field of recycling. And as we start getting involved in the intricacies of international and global co-operation, we must not forget the prime importance of the *small* community. Just as each one of us is less of an integrated and effective person if we try to smother (for whatever reason) the memories and lessons of our earlier life, so our civilisations, however complex, are not only poorer but doomed to disaster if their component 'bricks' are not healthy.

It is only by building with the bricks of community that we can foster cultural diversity which is necessary for biological diversity, as we saw in Chapter 3, and which is a basic precondition of a healthy society, as T. S. Eliot spelled out in *Notes Toward the Definition of Culture*. And cultural diversity only prospers if local communities have the power to make the decisions which most affect their own lives. Participation is not an add-on luxury but a basic ingredient of sustainability.

Schumacher has pointed out that if various factors including the speed of technical change work so that parents have nothing to teach their children and children nothing to accept from their parents, family life collapses and I suspect that most of us would agree that that is at least one factor in the present disintegration of urban life. To say that is not to deny that reverse generational education is a bad thing, but it must not become too dominant. Most of us are happy (and proud) if our children can help us to use our computers more efficiently, but if at an early stage they begin to think that we are totally incompetent in all the matters which make modern life tick, then a contempt sets in which, even if affectionate, destroys personal relationships. And a very important part of attempting to rebuild civilisation will be restoring family life as it is experienced in less 'advanced' societies. Visitors from fairly primitive cultures, like that of Ladakh in Kashmir, to so-called civilisation are are appalled by the way 'old people suffer, living alone with no one to talk to. Grandmothers may wait for months to see their grandchildren for a few short hours and then only get a small peck on the cheek'.

1 Jay Walljasper: 'Fine Villages of Finland' in *Resurgence* 174.
2 G. K. Chesterton: *The Napoleon of Notting Hill.*
3 *Ecological Economics* by The Group of Green Economists.
4 R. H. Tawney: *The Acquisitive Society.*
5 Kishore Mahbubani in *Foreign Affairs,* S/O 93.
6 *The Economist,* 2/09/95.
7 Readers will remember that in George Orwell's *1984* there was a permanent war between such blocs
8 UNRISD: *States of Disarray.*
9 Kennedy Graham in *The Planetary Interest.*
10 David C. Korten: 'The Taming of the Giants' in *Resurgence* 175.
11 David C. Korten: *When Corporations Rule the World,* p181.
12 Frances Moore Lappé in the *Ecological Economics Bulletin* 1/1.
13 Brewster Kneen: *Invisible Giant: Cargill and its Transnational Strategies.*

Chapter 12

What is true aid?

Real development cannot be purchased with foreign aid monies. Development depends on people's ability to gain control of and use effectively the real resources of their localities — land, water, labor, technology, and human ingenuity and motivation — to meet their own needs.

David C. Korten

Human Development is the end — economic growth a means.

Opening sentence of *Human Development Report 1996*

I F WE ARE to have a world which takes sustainable development seriously and accepts the necessity of working at all the various levels of community and national organisation which we explored in the last chapter, how are we to approach the question of aid to the poorer countries?

Clearly some help is going to be needed, starting from the present situation in a world where between 1960 and 1989 the percentage of global income absorbed by the richest twenty per cent of countries rose from 70% to 83% while that of the poorest 20% of countries fell from 2.3% to 1.4%.

The relative unimportance of money

Yet aid, equally clearly, cannot be measured in money alone, although we are so deeply embedded in this way of thinking that it is going to be difficult for us to escape. If every rich country in the world were to fulfil all its present monetary target pledges (which is inconceivable) the money as such would still make little difference to the poor of sub-Saharan Africa.

Nor does real aid consist only of gifts, although the right gifts can be useful. The wrong gifts however can be either useless or disastrous. When Aunt Miriam gives you cufflinks for Christmas, when you have long since finished wearing the kind of shirts which take cufflinks, it is a wrong gift, although kindly meant, because it is useless. When an advanced country tries to help a less advanced one by giving it complex machinery which suited its own economy but is now surplus to requirements (and the reason is always worth investigating) and which requires unobtainable backup and puts people out of work, it is a wrong gift — and not always kindly meant.

In the sustainable economy what we are always looking for is *wealth expressed in quality of life*. What we are not looking for is to maximise GNP, which would be about as sensible as maximising the number of notes in a symphony. But we probably should be involved in maximising human effort. Again, those who are old enough can remember the maximisation of human effort in World War II. William James suggested that we need a 'moral equivalent of war' and it may be that achieving a sustainable society is just that: 'the image of war without its guilt and only a very small percentage of its danger', to adapt Mr Jorrocks' definition of foxhunting.

(What fulfils this role when a sustainable society has been achieved is another but not unanswerable question).

Economic colonialism

We must find new lands from which we can easily obtain raw materials and at the same time exploit the cheap slave labour that is available from the natives of the colonies. The colonies would also provide a dumping ground for the surplus goods produced in our factories.

Cecil Rhodes

We have spoken already of the vital necessity of new markets for the old world. It is therefore to our very obvious advantage to teach the millions of Africa the wants of civilization so that, whilst supplying them, we may receive in return the products of their country and the labour of their hands.

Lord Lugard, Governor of Nigeria

The IMF, the World Bank, GATT and now the WTO were all founded for basically the same reasons as those quoted above. Lugard and Rhodes were relatively enlightened men and they and the founders of our modern international financial institutions also had other motives than purely commercial ones, such as the spread of 'civilisation'. They resembled Hilaire Belloc's Captain Blood who 'understood the native mind. He said "We must be firm but kind." A mutiny resulted'. But alas no mutiny has yet resulted to threaten the World Bank. It is simpler to brainwash the natives than to be forced into the position where 'Whatever happens we have got the Gatling gun and they have not!'[1] — although the institutions have in fact plenty of financial Gatling guns.

It would of course be wrong to portray colonialists or neo-colonialists as the unwitting tools of big business. They often knew (and know) what they were doing and believed it to be right, but the fact is that the institutions of neocolonialism have 'encouraged and coerced third world countries to lower [and abolish] their import quotas and tariffs which protected their fledgling industries, to devalue currencies making their exports cheaper and Western imports dearer, to cut welfare expenditure and to capitalise agriculture via Western machinery and agro-chemicals.'[2]

The special case of the Third World

The fundamental need of the Third World is the freedom to organise its own life. It has already more or less achieved freedom from overt colonial power. Freedom from the neocolonialism of the economic footprints it has not yet got. Nor has it got freedom from the tyranny of GATT and the other instruments of so-called free trade.

In particular, Third World countries are very likely to have got embroiled in a vicious spiral where they find themselves in debt to First World countries and then have to submit themselves to having their economies 'adjusted' by the World Bank. The results of this are often dramatic. 'In general, the primary incomes of the poor are down, the number of people living in poverty is up, and social income — access to public services — has decreased. Targeted interventions meant to protect the poor and vulnerable groups from the worst aspects of adjustment never reach all of the poor, and seldom reach most of the poor. Instead [in Africa] the major beneficiaries of adjustment have tended to be small groups of individuals with access to foreign exchange'. The World Bank has said that its work must be judged by the extent to which poverty can be said to be alleviated. Thus it stands condemned out of its own mouth.[3]

The priorities of the Third World need to be very different from those of the 'adjustments' wished upon them by the old economics. Their principal needs are 'acceleration of the transition to population stability; acceleration of the transition to renewable energy; education, training and employment creation, particularly for girls; technological transfer [to leapfrog the North's ecologically damaging industrial revolution] and job creation rather than automation; and direct poverty alleviation, including social safety nets and target aid'.[4]

We must not let fears of intellectual neo-colonialism prevent us from trying to offer help. If we do not encourage the Third World to feed itself sustainably, it will continue to feed itself unsustainably (for example by cut and burn) and the whole planet will suffer irremediable damage.

And it is absolutely vital that the economy of each nation (or bloc) is based on its ability to more or less feed itself. One of the most important measures of over-population is whether a country is any longer able to feed itself. By this standard Hong Kong is a monster, not an economic miracle, and the UK a poor country. Giving up feeding oneself in order to produce cash crops to balance one's trade can be fatal. Susan George quotes the example of

Senegal which 'borrowed heavily to install refining capacity for a million tonnes of groundnuts. But the soils are so depleted by groundnut production that today it can produce nowhere near that amount. Still, the cost of the industrial plant must be reimbursed — through exports of groundnuts.'

An end to free trade

It is not true that the most obvious thing for a man who has plucked an apple from an apple tree is to put it on a train and send it to the opposite side of England. The most obvious thing is to put it in his mouth.

G. K. Chesterton

I sympathise with those who would minimize, rather than with those who would maximize, economic entanglement between nations... Let goods be homespun whenever it is reasonably and conveniently possible, and above all, let finance be primarily national.

John Maynard Keynes

Free-trade agreements like NAFTA and GATT are not really trade agreements at all. They are economic integration agreements intended to guarantee the rights of global corporations to move both goods and investments wherever they wish — free from public interference or accountability.   David Korten, *New Internationalist*, April 1996

In a world which takes conservation of energy seriously, and a sustainable world has to do that, there is an immediate presumption against transporting large quantities of goods over long distances. (According to a report from SAFE it takes a litre of diesel to process and transport 10 litres of orange juice.) Because the presumption is strongest where the need for such transport is weakest, it is not surprising that the trade in cut flowers is one which has come under serious attack. The uninstructed observer might think that particular trade a rather small matter, but it is not so. A single Dutch company charters twelve Boeing 707s for flights from Nairobi to Amsterdam each week.[5] Who needs this trade? The answer is complex and interesting. The buyers do not fundamentally need an industry of this size and complexity. You and I when we 'want' cut flowers for our living room or to send to a friend in hospital would be quite happy to pluck them from our gardens if we had them, or to use a shop which bought from small market gardens round the towns in which we or the recipients live. We are capable of understanding that in winter they will cost more or may have to be artificial. We would not feel that civilisation was collapsing if we had to indulge in substitution and send something else instead.

No, the people who need the trade are not the consumers but the governments of Kenya and Ethiopia who grow the flowers. And they 'need' (usually foreign) companies to grow flowers on their best agricultural land, where their people could be growing food to feed themselves and the inhabitants of their cities, so they can export them to earn hard currency to pay for the debts that they have accumulated either from imports or aid. On the whole the poor do not need imports. And therefore they do not need exports. Japan, Korea and Taiwan all started their economic climb, not by exporting but by achieving high adult literacy and basic education, by radical land reform to create a thriving rural economy based on small farm production, and by supporting the development of rural industries that produced things needed by small farm families. The exports came later.

In Colombia they have a great success story with their new cut flower industry. This has an additional benefit for the economy in that the rather dicey statistics of the industry, which are unusually open to manipulation owing to the perishableness of the goods, provides an easy way of laundering drug money. 'When you see a small flower farm with a palace like house and the guy is vague about his other business ventures, you just know'.[6] In all these countries the flowers are grown by the most intensive of methods, with the expected effects on the soil and on the health of the workers who are often handling toxic pesticides with the minimum of precautions. (In 1992 farmers in Kenya were using such carcinogenic chemicals as Carbosulfan 25ec, banned in the US and elsewhere.) There is also an enormous drain on water supplies.

This is just one extreme example. There are plenty of others. A recent trade war between Canada and Italy over pasta was almost as absurd as the flying of American 'Danish pastries' to Scandinavia: not quite, since in the latter case a faxed exchange of recipes would have answered any problem that there was, while with pasta there is the complication that Canadian durum wheat is the best for the purpose. Another case is the inability recently recorded to buy any except Spanish asparagus in supermarkets in the Vale of Evesham.

The fact is that free trade benefits the elites in all countries but does not benefit the poor. Elites in Africa invest in high input production of cut flowers in order to sell them to elites in Europe. The myth that free trade benefits the poor is only true for rich countries where the cost of growing food has risen with wages and where, therefore, imported food is cheaper. And since the poorer you are the greater proportion of your money you spend on food, free trade benefits the urban proletariat while ruining the agricultural community, as happened in the UK. For it pays the elites to help the urban proletariat since that is where the votes are. A friend of mine reckoned some twenty years ago when he represented one of them that there were only three constituencies left in England where the farming (as opposed to the rural) vote made a decisive difference.

In fact we are conned into thinking that the most important factor in the economic life of our countries is trade by the myth of international competitiveness which, we are told, is the only thing which ensures the growth of our living standards. Unlike some myths, this one is just untrue. The growth rate of living standards (for the US, EU and Japan) essentially equals the growth rate of simple domestic productivity.[7]

GATT is of course far from universal in its application, whatever its devotees may claim. For instance it excludes the arms trade, dominated by the industrialised countries: military expenditure is allowed to be subsidised.

GATT also now includes an important extension of the rules protecting patents to include patents on products themselves as well as on the method of producing those products. This means that if someone designs a new technique for producing a drug more cheaply, they cannot use it because they thereby violate the patent. This is a serious deterrent to technical innovation and a massive protection for existing companies.[8]

The dogma of free trade pervades the world economy today. Its essence is that free and untrammelled trade leads to the best possible investment of resources and that any form of protective tariff leads to inefficiency. Recently however, in spite of the triumphs for free trade of a worldwide GATT agreement (or possibly because of them) even the hitherto most unchallenged arguments for it have come under attack.

For instance it was taken as unchallengeable that protected industries became weak, inefficient and brakes on progress. However the Research Director of the Economic Strategy Institute has recently pointed out that the protection under Reagan of the American automobile, steel, machine tool, semiconductor and textile industries actually helped to revitalise those sectors. It was long assumed that protected businessmen would fritter away their gains in large lunches. Instead, they seized a breathing space to bring their businesses up to date.

Defenders of free trade who find themselves well-suited for the moment by regional free trade blocs often find themselves arguing that regional trading pacts foster freer world trade. This is a very dubious proposition. General de Gaulle never favoured free trade. He was in favour of Community Preference and one of his problems in considering whether to let Britain in to the EEC was whether she could accept this.[9]

Appropriate technology

So, in order to combat this damaging myth of free trade one of the first things that is needed is to help poor countries to discover what is truly important for them and what is not. Labour-saving machinery is not: they have labour in abundance. What they need to be offered or given is intermediate or 'appropriate' technology. There are many examples of this, one being the small-scale production of salt by women's co-operatives in Sierra Leone.[10] And it should be emphasised that intermediate technology can take out drudgery without diminishing employment But a proper regard for appropriate technology is sometimes frustrated even by aid agencies. As Frances Cairncross of *The Economist* has commented acerbically: 'Agencies have budgets to spend and experts to employ'.

Nor is biotechnology necessarily appropriate. Dr Vandana Shiva, Director of the Research Foundation for Science, Technology and National Resource Policy in India, worries that in her own country upwards of 95% of the farm population could be displaced in the coming century by the biotechnology revolution in agriculture. If that were to happen, warns Shiva, there will be widespread social problems resulting in the kind of violence which has erupted in Yugoslavia.

And even the corporation as we know it may be inappropriate. I have already pointed out the fundamental dishonesty of the limited liability company. If we are to get away from that — and we must — perhaps we should take a large step and encourage the community-owned firm, which as Gar Alperowitz has pointed out, of its nature internalises its externalities. If it chooses to pollute, it is polluting itself and bears the costs.[11]

The spread of free trade, with its paradoxical corollary of the power to patent practically anything, has a considerable effect on biodiversity. Some botanical institutes, including those in New York and at Kew Gardens, have insisted that royalties for any commercially useful discoveries of plant research carried out on behalf of large companies should be paid to the countries from which the genetic material comes. That is by no means an ideal solution, and a way ought to be found of marrying the important principle that knowledge should be freely disbursed to the need to provide incentives for the work that needs to be done to explore new resources, whether found in tropical forests or dreamed up by people.

There is no reason why, if the world so chooses, the WTO, whose job it is for the main part to administer GATT, should not have in its charter a clause which was in the charter of its stillborn parent the International Trade Organisation. This would have allowed exceptions to free trade for measures taken in pursuance of any governmental agreement which relates solely to the conservation of fisheries resources, migratory birds or wild animals.[13]

Conserving resources

One of the things that is important is conservation of resources. Most people who live by the land or sea in communities understand that: the important thing is not to bribe them with high prices to break their own rules. Deep sea fishing, which at the moment is appallingly badly policed,[14] should be submitted to stringent controls as one way of preserving the small scale community-supporting fisheries of poor (and other) countries, since according to the FAO all the world's major fishing grounds are at or beyond their sustainable limits.[15]

Yet another way of helping poor countries and the environment at the same time is to recognise the economic values of wildlife and wetlands, as has successfully been done in Kenya, Zimbabwe, Malaysia and Peru,[16] although it must be emphasised that this is merely an interim accommodation to the old economics.

As regards the most important conservation property of all, energy, it is unrealistic in most parts of the world to envisage going suddenly over to using only renewables — but the depletion rate of non-renewables should not exceed the rate at which renewables can be substituted (the so-called Serafian rule).

Education and training

At present aid is often made dependent on cuts in public expenditure, usually in exactly the wrong places. It also tends to be directed towards capital investment which is simpler to administer and more visible afterwards, but small fragile communities do not have the capacity or need to absorb large projects. What they do need is the more cost-effective investment in people and skills and especially support in the early stages.

Any civilised employment of people involves them understanding their job. 'A system based entirely on the division of labour is in one sense literally half-witted', as Chesterton has pointed out. Fritz Schumacher indicated that we have had plenty of opportunity to observe since World War II the importance of education, training and morale which have produced so many 'economic miracles'.

Another way of helping poor countries ecologically is by funding appropriate project appraisals with a full review of all possible costs. And then, if outside operators have to be brought in, they should be made to post a bond equal to the current best estimate of the largest potential future environmental cost — a reversal of capitalism whereby the past pays for the future.

And it is important that, as far as possible, financing should be local. The Bangladesh bank which lends small sums to poor women at standard interest rates and which is being widely copied in the Third World has tiny default rates (large Western Banks please note).

1   Hilaire Belloc: *The Modern Traveller.*
2   'Beating back Predatory Trade', in *Foreign Affairs* 73/4
3   UNRISD/UNDP: *Adjustment, Globalisation and Social Development.*

4   Goodland: *Population, Technology and Lifestyle*.
5   Niala Maharaj and Gaston Dorren: *The Game of the Rose* (International Books), p39.
6   *Ibid* p54.
7   Paul Krugman: 'Competitiveness: A Dangerous Obsession' in *Foreign Affairs* M/A 94.
8   Noam Chomsky in *Resurgence* 173.
9   James Goldsmith: *The Response*, p32.
10 Intermediate Technology Group (HA/JM March 95).
11 'It's the System' in *The Ecological Economics Bulletin* Vol 1 No 2.
12 Frances Cairncross: *Green Inc.*
13 David Pepper: *Eco Socialism*.
14 Prof John Beddington of the Renewable Resources Group at Imperial College, London, quoted in *The Times* 14/09/95.
15 *World Watch Paper 126.*
16 *Blue Print 2*, pp196-7.

Chapter 13

The way forward for the world

He worships at the altar of the Free Market... But what kind of ethical social system take as its fundamental precepts the words 'I' 'me' and 'mine'? Our two year olds start like that and we spend the next twenty years trying to teach them that there's more than that to life.

Scott Turow: *Pleading Guilty*

It's no small thing! ye maun lie bare and hard...and you shall sleep with your hand upon your weapons. Aye, man, ye shall taigle many a weary foot or we get clear. But if ye ask what other chance ye have, I answer: Nane.

Alan Breck Stewart in R. L. Stevenson: *Kidnapped*

Politics is not the art of the possible. It consists of choosing between the disastrous and the unpalatable.

J. K. Galbraith

We do not so much move 'forward', as clear the mess and seek exit from the havoc perpetrated by the things we did yesterday.

Zygmunt Bauman

WE CAN POSSIBLY find some kind of a consensus on what is the way forward.

To start with there is wider agreement than one might suppose on the position in which we find ourselves. The late Jean Gimpel in his book *The End of the Future* and I reach much the same conclusion. We both see that this particular 'civilisation' in which we were brought up is coming to an end and we both agree that this is because capitalism and technology is being strangled by ecology. He seems to think that is a bad thing; I think it is the best thing that has happened in two millennia. It is always an interesting sign when ideological opponents agree on their diagnoses.

Prescriptions will of course differ, and we must look at some of the arguments against our own.

'Ecology is bad for profits'

The cruder apologists for capitalism can usually be defeated without too much trouble. Take for example the manager in Conrad's *Heart of Darkness* who deplored the fact that his agent Kurz's methods, including the display of the heads of natives on the walls of his stockade, had 'ruined the district' for ivory harvesting. It is not that people have given up thinking those thoughts, and those of Lugard and Rhodes quoted earlier: it is merely that hypocrisy (the homage paid by vice to virtue) and genuine progress have between them made their expression unacceptable. It's an early sign of the coming change!

And of course ecology is not bad for profits; study after study has shown that the ecological pioneer, exercising reasonable caution, can make her or his convictions profitable in anything except the shortest term.

'It will last our lifetime'

> Humbug, like flu, is extremely common.
>
> Mary Midgley

Again this is too cynical an argument to be deployed openly, but it is the more potent in that, unlike the last argument, it may well be true. But it is an unusual human being who feels no responsibility for their children and future generations, and the main way of tackling such selfishness is to point out that we are not talking about distant generations. It *may* last this person's lifetime but possibly only just. The menace that we are talking about is like the weed on the pond whose menacing daily doubling we described earlier.

It seems likely that it will be the USA which will be the last country to be converted to ecological thought, not because there are not plenty of people there with their hearts, minds and wills in the right place but because the people as a whole have lived their entire history on one frontier or another and it seems to them impossible that there is no more space for them to conquer. It is all part of the syndrome which makes them keep their right to carry guns in spite of the clearly proven arguments in favour of banning them. Variations on this argument are deployed by those science fiction fans who persist in pursuing the chimera of colonising (and presumably ruining) other planets and by those mystics such as Teilhard de Chardin who expect God to produce something better than humans. There is no way of proving their hopes false and God knows (as presumably he does) that we could do with something better, but for the time being we have got to cope with the problems we have with the tools at our disposal.

Governments are also problems. Those people who reach high office are not trained to deal with total paradigm changes and will continue to think that they can cope with the problems that confront them by means of incremental mechanical measures without seeing that what is needed is a change which will turn us from concern with quantity to concern with quality of life. A number of men and women of goodwill and competence in all political parties and none fall into this category.

'The way to sustainability is through deregulation and trade'

> The race is on ... to give the invisible hand of free-market economics a green thumb.
>
> E. O. Wilson

'Of course we must be sustainable. But sustainability demands efficient economies which imply deregulation and trade: anything else is inefficient'. So say the businessmen, but William Rees of the University of British Columbia has pointed out that total consumption by the human economy already exceeds national incomes; humankind is liquidating natural capital and thereby destroying our real wealth-creating potential. Efforts to expand our way to sustainability can only accelerate global decline and what is efficient in market terms is almost always costly and damaging in other ways — to employment, to social cohesion and to the environment.[1]

'You can't put the clock back'

This is a very deep-seated belief and needs more than Chesterton's riposte that 'Yes, you can. All you need to do is get on a chair and turn the hands' to be uprooted. For instance many people believe (sometimes regretfully) that 'globalisation is inevitable', but Dahrendorf et al in their *Report on Wealth Creation* suggest that in fact it is running out of steam. And the inhabitants of Tristan da Cunha took a five-year look at the modern world outside their island and voted to go back.

There are a number of allies who can be harnessed to help, some of them at first sight improbable. For instance the insurance industry is immensely powerful, having enormous sums to invest and representatives on the boards of most companies in the West. They are not going to rally to help industry to insure against the covering of the pond. If we are right in forecasting some of the perils of the future, insurance companies will be seeing them as clearly as we do and hedging their bets! Indeed, according to David Bellamy[2] the industry is active in initiating the restoration of 'meanders' on the Mississippi and the Upper Rhine in an effort to restore 'natural' flood control, destroyed by 'the axe of the spoiler and self-interest' which, in the words of John Clare, left 'a sicker brook, cold and chill'.[3]

We know that, as Karl Marx said, 'the nature which preceded human history today no longer exists anywhere', and it is only one hundred per cent ideologically pure Gaians who want to go back to such a position. The rest of us see some role for the human race.

There will be those who see the constraints which we will have to bear as some kind of eco-fascism. And there is of course that danger. China's population policy is not viewed with much favour by those brought up to treasure human rights. There will be a strong discipline enforced by circumstances but we can use the tools of Kerala rather than those of Beijing. (See Chapter 3.) It is clearly possible to contain many of the good effects of competition and individualism in 'game' situations within a framework of co-operation, and it ought likewise to be possible to contain individual freedom and cultural diversity within a framework of conformity to necessity.

What is certain is that a philosophy which values genetic diversity can be brought to value cultural diversity and will not share the view of the inhabitants of the Marshall Islands reputedly held by Henry Kissinger when they were likely to be affected by nuclear tests: 'There are only 90,000 of them out there: who gives a damn?'

Education will as always begin with the young. To start with they — unlike a lot of the rest of us — are inured to the fact that they need to learn. They are being taught from an early age by almost everybody that they must not always think 'I, I, I', and it will be some time before the world gets through with its message that their first instincts were right after all. (See Scott Turow above.) And finally it is the young who seem to sense instinctively that the ecological imperative is right.

If we are right in thinking that the path of ecological economics is the road that the world is bound to follow, the question remains as to whether it will go that way with the co-operation of most of humankind or forced by a series of devastating hammerblows from nature comparable to a cavalry charge by the Four Horsemen of the Apocalypse.

What are the targets?

If it is to go that way by consent a vast 'value-driven' propaganda campaign will be needed along the lines of that which persuaded Americans emerging from the inter-war recession that it was their duty to consume more. What will be the objectives of the campaign? Nicholas Georgescu-Roegen[5] has enumerated eight targets, each of which by itself is reasonable but which taken all together seem like asking for the moon. Nevertheless, I think that we all need to have them in mind and I list them here with my glosses in brackets:

(1) The abolition of all armaments. [This in fact is totally impossible. But not long ago the defence of Switzerland was said to depend on a militia of all citizens armed with rifles. And, obscene as it may seem to some, a combination of some such defence force at national levels with a UN nuclear deterrent might prove to be the ultimate answer — rather than the ultimate solution.]

(2) Assistance (rather than Aid!) to the poor countries to help them to

achieve self-sufficiency. [See Chapter 11.]

(3) The reduction of world population till it can be fed in its own countries by organic agriculture. [The one virtue of being able to use, at least temporarily, employment-saving technology is that it enables a shrinking young population to support a large aging one during the difficult transitional period.]

4) The strict control of non-renewable energy together with investment in non-renewable resources.

(5) An understanding that in a finite world, gadgetry is a vice [one to which I am grossly addicted].

(6) As is fashion [to which I am not!].

(7) The construction of as many goods as possible to be infinitely repairable.

(8) The realisation that saving time is only worthwhile if the use you are to put the time saved to is itself worthwhile [such as helping one's neighbour, achieving wisdom or producing good art].

The great advantage with which we start in this campaign is that, while being reasonable enough to woo the centre of politics, the Green cause already has strong roots in the thinking left and in the emotional right. The egalitarianism which is an inextricable part of the programme appeals to the left while the German Wandervogel and similar groups would have found themselves quite at home in a world of ideas about the conservation of nature, biological holism, nutritional purity, rural simplicity, energy efficiency, scarcity economics, strong regulation of industry and small-scale living which inform much of today's environmentalism.

The fact that we have a head start with the young does not mean however that we can afford to relax. The techniques of moral decision making have to be taught. Most people are not naturally empathetic and they have to learn to put themselves in other people's shoes. I read that children are being taught in a number of schools the techniques of mediation. These lessons are at least as important as literacy and numeracy and considerably more important than many other subjects. These are the techniques for living in community.

The role of establishments

But we must not underestimate the ability of 'establishments' to reform themselves at the same time as they are educating their electorates. I have already commented that the results of the Rio Summit could have been foretold by few people ten years before, and Andrew Ross's suggestion in 1994 that a paramilitary-environmental-industrial complex could emerge from the primitive military-industrial complex of the Cold War is not to be lightly dismissed.[6] I have already suggested that the ecological movement (in the spirit of the quotation from *Kidnapped* (above) may provide William James' 'moral equivalent of war'. It may be that the achievement of a sustainable society is just that.

Indeed if we are moving into a new paradigm it will have to be one in which there is greater peace than heretofore! The tendency to this will come with less poverty and more self-sufficiency but it will not come without difficulty. Britain for instance is heavily dependent for its balance of payments on its arms trade. This is neither very ethical nor economically healthy.

There is in the often seemingly muddled (but maybe merely tentative) thinking of those engaged on both sides of the battles to preserve or restore the rights of aboriginal peoples a growing acceptance of a diversity of cohabiting cultures which looks as if it might be very helpful to the new developments.

That is not to say that such accommodations will be easy. My wife's wanderings over the globe with exhibitions of contemporary British art brought me in touch with the fascinating problems which the inhabitants of St Helena are facing as they and the British Government try to decide whether they want to be exposed to the modern world or not.

But responsibility must be taken by those in power. That is not to say that solutions must be dictated from the centre. Far from it; the more the decisions come from the grassroots the better. But what cannot be dodged is that there is no way in which the care of the environment can be left to the 'invisible hand of the market place'. Frances Cairncross of *The Economist* winds up her book *Green, Inc.*, which is otherwise excessively kind to capitalist machinery, with a list of ten principles to be kept in mind by governments. The first is: 'Accept that the state of the environment is essentially government responsibility. A cleaner environment will not come about entirely as a result of unfettered market forces, any more than streets will be lit or criminals brought to justice'.[7] And Fred Hirsch suggested in *Social Limits to Growth* that where deliberate action cannot be used directly to legislate and enforce a change in individual motives and behaviour, 'it can be applied effectively and legitimately to removing obstacles to such a change'.

Moreover democracy provides the machinery to change for the whole of society those things which we do not have the guts to do on our own. This does not mean that we are enforcing on others that which we will not do ourselves; it means that we are joining with others to enforce on ourselves that which must be done.

The role of the individual

But what can the individual (or family) do to change things? John Seymour[8] has made a long list of which the following are some worthwhile practical items:

- boycott the National Lottery.
- patronise local small-scale shops.
- have as a family one less car than you think you need (remembering that if you live in a city you probably do not need a car at all and that it is considerably cheaper to hire a car when you really need one).
- refrain from buying goods brought from far away.
- encourage, support and initiate local credit and finance organisations.
- always support the local and the smallscale even when it is more expensive. Remember that it is likely to be the fair cost that you are paying while the cheaper goods in the supermarkets are cheaper because they impose hidden costs on others.

And it may well be that Europe with its Christendom tradition has much to offer us. Certainly its Christian Democrat way of working is superior ethically to that of the Anglo-Saxon countries. So, in the next and final chapter we must examine some of the problems which are more peculiarly British (or, usually, English).

1 'Green Economics', *New Internationalist Keynote* 4/96.
2 In a talk to the All-Party Conservation Group at the Palace of Westminster 25/04/96.
3 John Clare: *Remembrances.*
4 *German Ideology.*
5 Nicholas Georgescu-Roegen: chapter on 'Energy and Economic Myths' in Daly and Townsend: *Valuing the Earth.*
6 Andrew Ross: *The Chicago Gangster Theory of Life* (Verso 1994).
7 Frances Cairncross: *Green, Inc.* (Earthscan).
8 *Resurgence* 173

Chapter 14

The way forward for Britain

We act as though comfort and luxury were the chief requirements of life, when all we really need to make us happy is something to be enthusiastic about.

Charles Kingsley

WHAT THEN IS Britain to do, both as a nation and as a part of Western Europe. Indeed, what am *I* to do?

Changing ourselves

And that is where it starts. In fact, the individual is not helpless, and has more power for good in a society which takes social action seriously than in one which believes that 'there is no such thing as society' and that we are merely competitive individuals. One person on their own is merely likely to prove the truth of Adlai Stevenson's quip that 'power corrupts but lack of power corrupts absolutely'. But no one with friends and colleagues is without the power to influence people.

It has been said that 'the concept of recycling has undergone a transformation little short of miraculous, from the crazed gleam in the eye of a greenie to a moral imperative and a national habit'.[1] But it was the 'greenie with a crazy gleam in his (or her) eye' who set the ball rolling.

And power is not merely with the already rich or influential people. While we must not underrate the power of individuals we must not overrate the power (or at least the likely power) for good of those who are given a head start. History is full of rich men who have benefited mankind but it is even fuller of rich men who have harmed it. For every Andrew Carnegie endowing literacy and education there is at least one Robert Maxwell or Clarence Hatry and thousands of lesser lights who have cared only for themselves and their immediate families and have done immeasurable (and sometimes) unthinking harm on the way. And there have even been those like Cecil Rhodes[2] who did both good and harm in large measure.

But we can all of us have ideas and it is ideas which in the long run change the world. Jesus of Nazareth's influence is greater today than that of the

Emperor Tiberius. Lenin achieved a lot but Marx's economic diagnosis (if not his cures) will last longer.

And the first step towards changing the world is almost always to change ourselves. Everyone is more or less a hypocrite and indeed a certain amount of hypocrisy is essential. As the Duc de la Rochefoucauld remarked in his *Maxims* it is the 'homage paid by Vice to Virtue'.[3] But although hypocrisy may be a necessary stage in our own progression, it does not usually persuade others, and if we believe that the economy of the world must be sustainable, we must do our best at least to be moving in that direction ourselves. This involves our own conversion and our consciously trying to spread the message to others.

Our conversion will both start and be less painful if we are honest with ourselves about what it is we really want. Dr Robert Constanza has drawn up a short list of Real Wants and what in fact we settle for:[4]

Real wants	Settle for
Self esteem	Fancy car
Serenity	Drugs
Health	Medicine
Human happiness	GNP
Permanent prosperity	Unsustainable growth

The process of evangelism is a tricky one and not to be achieved merely by buttonholing strangers and asking them 'Are you saved?', 'Are you green?' The early Christians gained converts because they were seen to love one another. We will gain green converts if we are seen to go out of our way to conserve, to spend money rather than throw things away, to pay the full price for our food rather than a price artificially lowered by the despoliation of the Third World, and to enjoy doing it.

Local councils such as Sutton, Adur and Richmond have shown how green policies can be put into practice at a local level and by choosing the right people to send to parliament we can continue to green our approach to our country's problems. We in Britain do have some particularly tricky problems of our own, partly stemming, as we have seen, from our over-population. But others stem from a land tenure system which has given us landlordism instead of peasantry, and other historical inheritances from having been the world leaders in the agricultural and industrial revolutions and a major imperial power.

Immediate political challenges

Protecting the poor

One of the most important problems before us is how to charge the full rate for resources without causing misery to the poor. A main objection to a switch from taxation of incomes (which is a tax on employment) to a tax on the use of resources is that the former is at least capable of being progressive (e.g. redistributive), though these days it usually is not, while the latter does not on the face of it seem to have that potentiality.

But there are ways round this problem. One is taxing the size and 'guzzling factor' of a car rather than petrol as such, which would protect the rural poor who need cars because there is little public transport. In the utility field (gas, electricity and water) a minimum quantity can be supplied at a low price with higher prices (possibly even steeply higher prices) above that level. Such policies should be accompanied by subsidy of energy efficiency .

Nor should there be any doubt at all that the development of environmentally sound industry is going to create a great many jobs and that the countries which realise this and have the political structure and willpower to cash in on it are going to be creating genuine wealth and work.[5]

But the task of protecting the poor, while moving along the path to giving them as near an equal vote in the market place (as opposed to the body politic wher they have one already) as can be managed, is a larger and more fundamental one than that of protecting them from the problems of environmental pricing. A good start is the Citizen's Income which produces a small guaranteed income for every citizen.[6]

Reducing the use of cars

Another fairly easy political step is to take every opportunity to subsidise friendly neighbourhood shopping habits as opposed to large space-hungry out-of-town hypermarkets. The ecologically wasteful methods of the latter range far beyond what is immediately apparent. At the moment food grown near Evesham goes to Hereford, Dyfed and Manchester before being sold in Evesham.[7]

In this area the new information super highway may help. The Henley Centre and the Institute of Directors predict that four in ten journeys will be replaced by 2010 by 'virtual travel' including on-screen shopping malls and interactive CD Rom.[7] This is an area where major steps will have to be taken to ensure that the poor, not owning computers, do not lose out once again. And the whole concept can hardly be classed as neighbourly.

Buying education

A particular problem which Britain faces is that its wide gap between rich and poor is supported by the class system reinforced by the private education system. We had a chance to solve that when the First Report of the Public Schools Commission reported back in the sixties. Alas, the usual determination of the ideologues in the Labour Party not to accept half a loaf on account meant that we received no bread. But the growing bankruptcy of Britain is now increasing the tendency to make decent education dependent on private wealth. It has now spread to the university system. It is very important for society to make sure that bought education does not necessarily give large monetary rewards, although Keynes did suggest on one occasion that high salaries are necessary in order to keep the psychological types who become tycoons from moving into organised crime! The evidence does not seem to show that it has had the required effect...

If, as is possible, the new information highway makes it more attractive to teach children at home — thus giving them the two years advantage over their contemporaries that evidence seems to suggest[8] — the poor are going to be at a disadvantage yet again, firstly through not being able to afford the equipment, and secondly through being caught in the cycle of deprivation with deprived parents being unable to teach their children adequately.

Another area which will cause particular problems for Britain is its countryside. No more trenchant example of the difference between ecology and environmentalism can be found. And for once this is a British, not merely an English problem: 'Scottish landowners [are] a selfish, ferocious, famishing, unprincipled set of hyenas,' said the MP Tom Johnston, and the history of the Scottish clearances are enough to support this trenchant judgement. Moving the economy into an ecological paradigm will shift a lot of activity out of the towns into the British countryside. The building up of rural life and the encouragement of small-scale mixed agriculture is not going to be popular with the Council for the Protection of Rural England and its Scottish equivalent.

But not all is gloom. The new paradigm will put a premium on the proper treatment of animals and that is an area where we start with an advantage. British latent humanitarianism and overt inventiveness ought to be able to make us a leader in reversing the trend towards factory farming of all kinds.

Another area in which we ought to be able to make our mark is in the field of art. A new ecological paradigm will automatically give us a new direction in art and one that may suit us. The aim will be to rescue the professionals from commercialism and introduce the amateurs to a proper professionalism! A tax and industrial system which provides leisure rather than unemployment and decouples income from work through such instruments as the Citizen's Income should do just that.

We also have the ability to use democracy in control of bureaucracy. Before the present debauchment of the civil service and its removal from democratic control through quangos, we used to have a model set-up. It may be that in a complex world certain powers must be given to bureaucrats which were not given before (such as giving the power to control inflation to a central bank) — but the ultimate power to decide fundamental policy must be in the hands of the voters.

And if we and our children are to live in a wealthy green (not a rich emerald) world, we must start out along the strait and narrow path today.

1   David Nicholson-Lord: 'The End of Consumerism' in *Earth Matters* 28.
2   Whatever one may think of Rhodes' colonial adventures, Stellenbosch botanical gardens and the Rhodes scholarships (in result if not in conception) were lasting achievements for good.
3   But it was Wilde, to whom that remark is often attributed, who in one of his stories for children tells the unforgettable tale of the man who wore a hypocrite's mask of good-will only to find that in the end his face and his life conformed to it.
4   'The Importance of Envisioning in Motivating Change Toward Sustainability' in *The Ecological Economics Bulletin* Vol 1 No 2.
5   For possibly the best resumé of a practical ecological political programme see Michael Jacobs: *Sustainability and Socialism* (SERA).
6   'Towards a New Social Compact: Citizens Income and Radical Tax Reform' by James Robertson in *The Political Quarterly* J/M 96.
7   Angela Paxton: *Food Miles*.
8   *The Times* 27/04/96.

BIBLIOGRAPHY

Abernethy, Virginia D.: *Population Politics* (Insight Books)

Ahmed, Zahir: *Land Reforms In South-East Asia* (Orient Longman 1975)

Albert, Michel: *Capitalism Against Capitalism* (Whurr 1993)

Athanasiou, Tom: *Divided Planet* (Little Brown 1996)

Bahro, Rudolf: *Avoiding Social and Ecological Disaster* (Gateway Books 1994)

Barbier, Edward B., Joanne C. Burgess and Carl Folke: *Paradise Lost?* (Earthscan 1994)

Barnaby, Frank and Rob Green: *Deterring War Responsibly* (Just Defence 1995)

Baum, Frank: *The Wonderful Wizard Of Oz* (1900)

Bauman, Zygmunt: *Alone Again* (Demos 1994)

Beaumont, Tim: (1) *The Yellow Brick Road* (Holystone Productions 1980)
(2) and John Pardoe: *Integration and Choice: A Liberal Plan for the Public Schools* (Prism Education Pamphlets)

Beckerman, Wilfred: *Small Is Stupid* (Duckworth 1995)

Berry, Thomas CP (with Thomas Clarke CJ) *Befriending the Earth* (Twenty-Third Publications: Mystic, Connecticut)

Bormann, F. H.: *Unlimited Growth?* (*Bioscience* Vol 22 No 12 pp706-9)

Bormann, F. H., Diana Balmori and Gordon Geballe: *Redesigning The American Lawn* (Yale University Press 1993)

Bormann, F. H. and Stephen R. Kellert: *Ecology, Economics, Ethics (The Broken Circle)* Yale University Press

Brown, Lester R. (1) and Hal Kane: *Full House* (W. W. Norton 1994)
(2) *Who Will Feed China?* (Worldwatch 1995)

Bunyard, Peter and E. Goldsmith: *Gaia, The Thesis, The Mechanism And The Implications* (1988)

Cairncross, Frances: *Green Inc* (Earthscan 1995)

Cameron, James, Paul Demaret and Damien Geradin: *Trade and The Environment: The Search For Balance* (Cameron and May)

Cavanagh, John, John Gershman, Karen Baker and Gretchen Helmke: *Trading Freedom* (Institute For Food and Development Policy USA

Chesterton, G. K.: *The Napoleon Of Notting Hill* 1904
The Outline Of Sanity 1926

Child Poverty Action Group: *Off The Map: Social Geography of Poverty* (CPAG 1995)

Clifford, Paul Rowntree: *Radical Politics* (The Yard Press 1996)

Club Of Rome: *Limits To Growth* (1972)

Cobb, Clifford, Ted Halstead and Jonathan Rowe: 'If The Gdp Is Up Why Is America Down?' (*The Atlantic Monthly* 10.95)

Cohen, Joel E.: *How Many People Can The Earth Support?* (W. W. Norton 1996)

Cooper, Richard N.: *Environmental And Resource Policies For The World Economy* (Brookings Institute 1994)

Cooper, Tim: *Beyond Recycling; The Longer Life Option* (New Economics Foundation)

Cruttwell, Peter C.: *History Out Of Control* (Green Books 1995)

Dahrendorf, Ralf : (1) *Life Chances* (Weidenfeld/University of Chicago Press 1979)

(2) et al: *Report On Wealth Creation and Social Cohesion In A Free Society* (CWCandSC 1995)

Daly, Herman E.:(1) and Townsend, Kenneth N. (eds.): *Valuing The Earth: Economics, Ecology, Ethics* (MIT Press 1993). Expanded edition of *Toward A Steady State Economy* (W. H. Freeman 1973) including Paul and Anne Ehrlich on Population, Nicholas Georgescu-Roegen on Entropy, Garrett Hardin on The Tragedy Of The Commons, E. F. Schumacher on The Age Of Plenty: a Christian View and Buddhist Economics, C. S. Lewis on The Abolition Of Man

(2) 'Boundless Bull' (in *Gannett Centre Journal* and *Resurgence* 175)

(3) see also Goodland

Dasgupta, Partha: (1) *An Inquiry Into Well-Being and Destitution* (Clarendon Press 1993)

(2) 'Population, Resources, Knowledge And Destitution: The Making Of An Economist' in *Makers Of Modern Economics, Vol 1*, ed Arnold Heertje (Harvester Wheatsheaf 1993)

Douthwaite, Richard: *Short Circuit* (Green Books 1996)

Durkhein, Emil: *Suicide* (London 1952)

Ehrlich, Paul and Anne: See Daly (1)

Eliot, T. S.: *Notes Towards The Definition Of Culture* (Faber 1948)

Esty, Daniel C.: *Greening The GATT* (Institute For International Economics 1994)

European Environmental Almanac (Earthscan 1995)

Eurostat Yearbook 1995

Evans, Stanley G.: *The Social Hope Of The Christian Church* (Hodder and Stoughton 1965)

Fairlie, Simon: *Low Impact Development* (Jon Carpenter 1996)

Falk, Richard: *On Human Governance* (Polity Press 1995)

Ferre, Frederick and Peter Hartel (eds): *Ethics And Environmental Policy* (University of Georgia 1994)

Fowler, Cary and Pat Mooney: *The Threatened Gene* (Lutterworth Press 1990)

Gardner, Howard: *Multiple Intelligences* (Basic Books 1993)

Garrett, Laurie: *The Coming Plague* (Virago 1995)

Georgescu-Roegen, Nicholas: see Daly (1)

Gibson, William: (1) *Neuromancer* (Gollancz 1984)

    (2) *Count Zero* (Gollancz 1986)

    (3) *Mona Lisa* (Gollancz 1988)

Gimpel, Jean: *The End Of The Future* (Adamantine Press Ltd 1995)

Goldsmith, Edward: (1)*The Way: An Ecological World View* (Rider 1992)
    See also Bunyard and Goldsmith

Goodland R., H. Daly and S. El Serafy (Ed): *Population, Technology and Lifestyle* (Island Press, Washington 1992)

Gore, Al: *The Earth In Balance* (Earthscan 1992)

Gorringe, Timothy J.: *Capital and The Kingdom* (Orbis/SPCK 1994)

Gotlieb, Yosef: *Development, Environment And Global Dysfunction* (St Lucie Press 1996)

Graham, Keenedy: *The Planetary Interest* (Global Security Programme: Occasional Paper No 7 1995)

Gray, John: (1) *Beyond The New Right* (Routledge 1993)

    (2) *After Social Democracy* (Demos 1996)

Green, Damian: *Communities In The Countryside* (Social Market Foundation 1996)

Group Of Green Economists, The: *Ecological Economics* (Zed Books 1992)

Hardin, Garrett: see Daly (1)

Harrison, Paul: *The Third Revolution* (I. B. Tauris London and St Martin's Press NY)

Harvey, Graham: *The Killing Of The Countryside* (Jonathan Cape 1997)

Henderson, Hazel: *Building A Win-Win World* (Berrett-Koehler 1996)

Hirsch, Fred: *Social Limits To Growth* (Routledge and Kegan Paul 1977)

Herring, Ronald J.: *Land To The Tiller* (Yale University Press 1983)

Hobsbawm, Eric: *Age Of Extremes* (M Joseph 1994)

Hollis, Christopher: (1) *Death Of A Gentleman* (Burns and Oates 1943 and Fontana)

    (2) *The Mind Of Chesterton* (Hollis and Carter 1970)

House Of Lords Select Committee On Science and Technology: *Fish Stock Conservation and Management 1995-6*

House Of Lords Select Committee On Sustainable Development, HL 72 (HMSO 1995)

Huntington, Samuel P.: 'The Clash Of Civilisations' (*Foreign Affairs* Summer 1993 et seq)

Hutton, Will: *The State We're In* (Jonathan Cape 1995)

Independent Commission On Population And Quality Of Life: *Caring For The Future* (OUP 1996)

Jacobs, Michael: *Sustainability and Socialism* (SERA 1995)

Jansson, Annmari, Monica Hammer, Carl Folke and Robert Constanza: *Investing In Natural Capital* (ISEE and Island Press 1994)

Johnson, Paul and Howard Reed: *Two Nations: The Inheritance Of Poverty and Affluence* (Institute For Fiscal Studies: 1996)

Kneen, Brewster: *Invisible Giant: Cargill And Its Transnational Strategies* (Pluto Press and Fernwood Publishing)

Korton, David C.: *When Corporations Rule The World* (Kumarian Press 1995)

Kung, Hans: *Judaism* (SCM Press 1991)
  Christianity (SCM Press 1994

Lang, Tim and Colin Hines: *The New Protectionism* (1993)

Leopold, A.: *A Sand Country Almanack* (Ballantine Books 1970)

Lewis, C. S.: *The Abolition Of Man* (Oxford University Press 1943)

Lind, Michael: *The Next American Nation* (The Free Press 1995)

Lovelock, J. E.: (1) *Gaia: A New Look At Life On Earth* (OUP 1979)
  (2) 'The Gaia Hypothesis' in Bunyard and Goldsmith

Macgillivray, Alex and Simon Zadek: *Accounting For Change* (NEF 1995)

Macintyre, Alisdair: *After Virtue* (Duckworth 1985)

Maharaj, Niala and Gaston Dorren: *The Game Of The Rose* (International Books 1995)

Marris, Robin: *How To Save The Underclass* (Macmillan Press/St Martin's Press 1996)

Massingham, H. J.: *The Small Farmer* (Collins 1947)

Meade, James: *Full Employment Regained?* (Cambridge University Press 1996)

Mellert, Robert B.: *What Is Process Theology? The Thought Of Alfred North Whitehead* (Paulist Press 1975)

Moggridge, D. E.: *Keynes* (Fontana Modern Masters 1976)

Miller, Walter M. Jr: *A Canticle For Liebowitz* (Weidenfeld and Nicolson/Black Swan 1960)

Mulgan, Geoff and Robin Murray: *Reconnecting Taxation* (Demos 1993)

Myers, Isabel Briggs and Peter Myers: *Gifts Differing* (Consulting Psychologists Press 1980)

Myers, Norman (ed): *Gaia Atlas Of Planet Management* (Gaia Books 1984, rev ed 1993)

Nader, Ralph et al: *The Case Against Free Trade: Gatt, NAFTA and The Globalisation Of Corporate Power* (1993)

Norberg-Hodge, Helena: *Ancient Futures, Learning From Ladakh* (Rider 1991)

North, Richard D.: *Life On A Modern Planet* (Manchester University Press 1995) (partly funded by ICI)

O'Riordan, Tim (ed): *Ecotaxation* (Earthscan 1997)

O'Riordan, Tim and James Cameron (eds): *Interpreting The Precautionary Principle* (Earthscan 94)

Ockenden, Jonathan and Michael Franklin: *European Agriculture* (a Chatham House Paper: Pinter 1995)

Oppenheim, Carey and Lisa Harker: *Poverty, The Facts* (CPAG 1996, 3rd ed)

Ormerod, Paul: *The Death Of Economics* (Faber 1994)

Osborne, Lawrence: *Restoring The Vision* (Mowbray 1995)

Painter, Michael and William H. Durham: *The Social Causes Of Environmental Destruction In Latin America* (University of Michigan Press 1995)

Papworth, John: *Small Is Powerful* (Adamantine Press 1995)

Parker, Hermione: *Instead Of The Dole* (Routledge 1991)

Paxton, Angela: *The Food Miles Report* (Safe Alliance 1994

Pearce, David et al: (1) *Blueprint For A Green Economy* (Earthscan 1989)

   (2) *Blueprint 2: Greening the World Economy* (Earthscan 1991)

   (3) *Blueprint 4: Capturing Global Environmental Value* (Earthscan 1995)

   (4) *Economic Values and The Natural World* (Earthscan 1993)

   (5) *Sustainable Development* (Edward Elgar 1990)

   See Turner and J. J. Warford: *World Without End* (Oxford University Press 1993)

Pepper, David: *Eco-Socialism* (Routledge 1993)

Philo, Chris (ed): *Geography Of Poverty In The UK* (see especially Doreen Massey and John Allen: 'High Tech Places: Poverty In The Midst Of Growth')

Pizzigati, Sam: *The Maximum Wage* (Apex Press 1992)

Pretty, Jules N. and Rupert Howes: *Sustainable Agriculture In Britain* (IIED Research Series 2/1)

Prugh, Thomas et al: *Natural Capital And Human Economic Survival* (ISEE Press 95)

Raven, John: *The New Wealth Of Nations* (Royal Fireworks Press and Bloomfield Books 1995)

Rawls, J.: *A Theory Of Justice* (Oxford University Press 1972)

Real World Coalition: *The Politics Of The Real World* (Earthscan 1996)

Reid, David: *Sustainable Development: An Introductory Guide* (Earthscan 95)

Ross, Andrew: *The Chicago Gangster Theory Of Life* (Verso 1995)

Roszak, Theodore: *The Voice Of The Earth* (Bantam Press 1993)

Rowell, Andrew: *Green Backlash* (Routledge 1996)

Royal Commission On Environmental Pollution: various reports (HMSO)

Ruskin, John: (1) *Unto This Last*

   (2) *Essays On Political Economy*

Russell, Hilary: *Poverty Close To Home* (Mowbray 1995)

Sachs, Wolfgang: (1) (ed): *Global Ecology* (Zed Books 1993)
   (2) (ed): *Development Dictionary* (Zed Books 1992)
Sale, Kirkpatrick: *Rebels Against The Future* (Addison-Wesley 1995)
Schumacher, E. F.: (1) *Small Is Beautiful* (Abacus 1974)
   (2) *A Guide For The Perplexed* (Abacus 1977)
   (3) *Good Work* (Jonathan Cape 1979)
   (4) see Daly (1)
Sen, Amartya: *Resources, Values and Development* (Blackwell)
Shiva, Vandana: *Monocultures Of The Mind* (Zed Books and Third World Network 1993)
Simmons, David: *Reinventing The Economy* (Jon Carpenter 1996)
Simons, Robert G.: *Competing Gospels: Public Theology And Economic Theory* (E. J. Dwyer 1995, distributed by Columba Book Service)
Tansey, Geoff and Tony Worsley: *The Food System* (Earthscan 1995)
Tawney, R.H: *The Acquisitive Society* (Fabian Society 1920)
Thompson, E. P.: *The Making Of The English Working Class* (Penguin 1963)
Toffler, Alvin: *Future Shock* (Collins 1980)
Tomlinson, Dave: *The Post-Evangelical* (SPCK Triangle)
Trainer, Ted: *Towards A Sustainable Economy* (Jon Carpenter 1996)
Turner, R. Kerry with David Pearce and Ian Bateman: *Environmental Economics (An Elementary Introduction)* (Harvester Wheatsheaf 1994)
United Nations Development Programme: *Human Development Report* (OUP 1996)
United Nations Research Institute For Social Development: (1) *States Of Disarray* (UNRISD 1995)
   (2) *Adjustment, Globalisation And Social Development* (UNRISD 1995)
Wackernagel, Mathis and William Rees: *Our Ecological Footprint* (New Society Publishers 1996, distributed by Jon Carpenter)
Weizsacker, E. U. von: *Earth Politics* (Zed Books 1994)
Wesker, Arnold: *Their Very Old And Golden City* (Penguin New Dramatists 10 1967)
Whitehouse, Alfred North: see Mellert, Robert B.
Wicksteed, Philip: *The Common Sense Of Political Economy* (Routledge 1933)
Wilson, A. N.: *Hilaire Belloc* (Hamish Hamilton 1984)
World Commission On Environment and Development: *Our Common Future* ('The Brundtland Report') (Oxford University Press 1987)
World Resources Institute, UNEP, UNDP and World Bank: *World Resources 1996-1997* (OUP 1996)
Worldwatch Institute: all the Worldwatch Papers, especially no. 126, Hilary F. French:*Partnership For The Planet*
Zadek, Simon and Christian Haas: *Dangerous Trading* (The Dryden Press 1995)

INDEX

The Power in Our Hands

Neighbourhood based, world shaking

Tony Gibson

Tony Gibson matches the capacities of ordinary people doing extraordinary things with our prospects for survival. Drawing on countless historical and present-day examples of individuals and groups doing their own thing, pooling resources, re-writing the rules and saying Enough is enough! — from the Grameen Bank in Bangladesh to the Rochdale Pioneers, from Ken Saro-Wiwa to Tom Paine and Emma Must — he shows how the potential for change and success lies in basic human assets: the creative instinct to do things ourselves; the staying power that comes from working together on the same footing and sharing the credit; the inborn urge to ask why? and then how?; the support we get from family and community; and that great human asset, time on our hands.

He shows how too much talk gets in the way of practical action, and outlines ways to bring about changes, from the ground up; developing working relation-ships through which we can regain control of our lives, linking up with others, near and far, who bring the same basic human resources to bear on the problem / opportunity they face.

The book concludes with a discussion of working models for change at neigh-bourhood level and the working relationships they engender, drawing on the resourcefulness and willingness of ordinary people to improve their own lives and the condition of their neighbourhood.

"This book is invaluable... a joy. I find it inspiring... He hits his target and does so in a manner the reader can never forget." From the Foreword by Lord Scarman

"This is the missing link in the debate about how we live, the secret formula that our leaders consistently misunderstand, Tony Gibson's book is about people and power and how the grassroots can effect real change. It's vital!" John Vidal, *The Guardian*

£10 pbk 320pp illustrated 1 897766 28 9

On these pages we list some of the other titles we publish that are likely to be of interest to readers of this book. Any book may be purchased post free by sending a cheque/PO to Jon Carpenter Publishing, The Spendlove Centre, Charlbury OX7 3PQ. Credit card orders (p&p £1 per order) may be phoned to 01608 811969. A comprehensive free catalogue is also available: please ask for one.

Ethical Investment

A saver's guide
Peter Lang

The book for anyone with money to invest — whether a few hundred pounds, or many thousands — who tries to apply ethical standards to their everyday life, but who doesn't have a detailed understanding of money and investment. Written in everyday language, free of the jargon of the financial world.

Unlike the typical financial adviser, the author explains and describes all the ethical investment opportunities, including those that don't pay a commission to 'independent financial advisers' for recommending them. These include banks, building societies, and a number of funds and companies in the so-called 'social economy', as well as the commission-paying unit trusts, PEPs and pension funds. There is also a discussion of the choice of insurance companies.

Ethical Investment explains how all these various investments operate, their ethical pros and cons, and guides the investor through the questions that need to be asked before deciding whether to sign on the dotted line.

Peter Lang pulls no punches in revealing

• why 'independent' financial advisers are not independent in the way you might think

• why financial advisers are extremely selective in the investments they recommend

• why many investment opportunities sold as 'ethical' are far from ethical

• why pensions are unlikely to keep you in old age in the manner the brochures suggest

• why a pension may not give you the best income in retirement

• why the best investment for your future might be to spend rather than save

• how companies make massive deductions from the money you invest

• the widely differing ethical criteria used by different 'ethical' funds

• where to find the information you need to judge a company's ethical record

Peter Lang is an environmental consultant and writer. He is the author of *Lets Work: Rebuilding the local economy*, the definitive guide to setting up and running LETS (Local Exchange Trading Systems). He is currently helping set up Britain's first ethical property company.

£10 pbk   192pp illustrated   1 897766 20 3

Low Impact Development

Planning and people in a sustainable countryside
Simon Fairlie

This complete re-examination of Britain's planning system from the bottom up – from the point of view of the planned, rather than of the planner – is an important contribution to the topical debate about the future and use of the countryside and what it means to achieve sustainability in the modern world.

Simon Fairlie argues that instead of excluding low income people from living and working in rural areas, planners should look favourably on proposals for low impact, environmentally benign homes and workplaces in the open countryside. Criteria for planning approval at present favour the wealthy commuter and the large-scale farmer and discriminate heavily against (e.g.) smallholders, low-impact homes, and experimental forms of husbandry.

The book is the result of much detailed research. It includes a number of cases studies of low impact developments, some of which received permission, some of which failed. It includes illustrations; policy recommendations; guides to acts of parliament, government circulars and policy guidelines etc.; references; and explanatory appendices. It is an invaluable tool both for those who wish to live on the land in a sustainable manner, and for planners and politicians who would like to make it possible for them to do so. As well as proposing changes to planning law, the author shows how existing regulations can be used to enable many environmentally benign projects to take place.

Simon Fairlie is an editor of *The Ecologist*, and co-author of *Whose Common Future?* (Earthscan, 1993). He writes for *The Guardian, New Statesman and Society*, and *Perspectives*.

£10 pbk 176pp illustrated 1 897766 25 4

Reinventing the Economy

The Third Way
David Simmons

How Margaret Thatcher and, after her, John Major have traded on popular disil-
lusionment with socialism and a deliberate falsification of what Keynes was saying
to discredit the left-of-centre consensus in Britain today and impose an unjust
economic and social system that has but one objective: to re-allocate wealth from
the lower and middle income groups to the already wealthy, by making ninety per
cent of people worse off. This has been done at the expense of the job security
and welfare of the overwhelming majority.

The New Right cannot succeed in its claimed goal of creating wealth for all in
a competitive market economy, as it is neither interested in, nor relevant to, the
concerns of economic and social justice. Yet many people have come to believe
that because socialism has been discredited, the political philosophy of the New
Right is the only possible option.

Simmons' original contribution to contemporary economic debate is to show
that this is not true.

While other writers have set out to demonstrate the failure of the New Right,
Simmons goes further: he shows that since the Keynesian consensus did not fail,
but was merely replaced by politicians with different priorities, there is an alternative. This can be found in the nature of government itself in a liberal
democracy, in the consensus that already exists among voters, and in the example
of those countries where different strategies are in place and working successfully.
Liberal democracy, by definition, is concerned with the welfare of all. And among
the population at large, there is a clear consensus in favour of established left-of-
centre policies: the welfare state, government intervention in the economy,
Keynesian demand management and so on. The consensus is within the range of
traditional Labour policies, and any party offering an alternative to the New Right
should take this on board.

The evidence shows that this programme is proven to be effective in creating
a socially and economically healthy society.

"A powerful indictment of New Right policies." Professor Masato Oka,
Yokohama City University

David Simmons is a former Lecturer in Economics and the author of several
books. Economic Power was praised by Leopold Kohr for its 'careful scholarship,
the soundness of its economics'.

£11.99 pbk   288 pages 1 897766 17 3

Towards a Sustainable Economy

The need for fundamental change
Ted Trainer

A lucid and hard-hitting analysis of the truth about our economic system that explains precisely why a few people are getting richer, most people are getting poorer, and why – if we don't change our ways – we're all heading for global catastrophe. Mass poverty and hunger, unemployment, under-development, waste, armed conflict, resource scarcity and environmental destruction — all are caused by the disastrous flaws in our economy.

Ted Trainer shows how economic growth is seriously mistaken because it ignores finite resource and ecological limits, thereby promoting violence and injustice as well as ecological calamity.

Having invalidated both 'free enterprise capitalism' and 'big state socialism' as viable long-term economic systems, Dr Trainer puts forward an alternative, a Third Way 'conserver society' that includes some of the best elements of the other two. His argument is that an economy for a sustainable world order must involve simpler living standards, a high degree of local economic self-sufficiency and therefore much less transport and travel, a much smaller cash sector of the economy, more cooperative arrangements such as town banks and working bees, and many free goods from Permaculture-designed 'edible landscapes'.

The 'limits to growth' are as real as ever, and we ignore them at our peril.

Ted Trainer's previous books include *Abandon Affluence!* ("Spares no illusions" – *The Ecologist*) and *The Conserver Society* (both Zed Books) and *Developed to Death* (Green Print, now in its third printing).

£10.99 pbk 192pp 1 897766 14 9

No Change? No Chance!

The politics of choosing green
Jean Lambert

A longstanding participant in the European federation of green parties, Jean Lambert is uniquely qualified to write this introduction to the big issues of the day: poverty, community, global relationships, and ecological limits.

Written in everyday language, and jargon free, this book brings the essence of the green message home to every citizen, and looks at realistic ways we can overcome the problems that confront the human race.

Not another 'environmentalist' book, this is a bold account of the social, economic and political message of the green movement today.

Outline

I The political crisis
  How I got involved · Why bother?

II Why the system isn't coping
  Governments bound by dogma: ignoring the 'planet as provider' · Poverty: how maximising consumption does not meet people's needs · Community: privatisation of community spirit · The utilitarian emphasis in education · Global insecurity, and how free trade damages the local economy · Ecology: the new factor

III Where do we go from here?
  The new framework: sustainable development, meeting need, taking an international perspective · Tackling poverty: consuming less but better, new indicators of wealth, and developing the informal economy · Caring for communities: constitutional change, education for the whole person, new policies for health and social services, integrated planning, tackling crime · Getting the ecology right: agriculture and food, meeting energy needs, using less transport, cutting pollution · Global security: arms trade, ethical foreign policy, the future of the UN, the future of Europe

IV Tying it together
  The movement for change here and abroad · The growth of the greens as a positive force countering the nationalistic fear-driven politics of fascism · The values that underlie a green society: a future worth having

Jean Lambert is a teacher, a spokeswoman for the UK Green Party, and a former chair of its executive. She has conducted research for the European Parliament, and is on the council of Charter 88.

£7.99 pbk 128pp 1 897766 23 8